Answers
And More

BOOK TWO

The God Of Creation

Enjoying The Best That Life Has To Offer
With
Kenneth W. Howard, PhD

Published By
Direction Inc.
Established 1974
Middletown, Ohio

Copyright © 2001 by Kenneth W. Howard

All rights reserved. No part of this publication may be reproduced or transmitted in any form or by any means, electronic or mechanical, including photocopying, recording, or by any information storage or retrieved system, without written permission from Kenneth W. Howard and Direction, Inc (publisher), except for the inclusion of quotation in a review.

Direction, Inc.
PO Box 213
Middletown, Ohio 45042
e-mail   direct @ siscom.net

First printing 2001
ISBN: 0-9703777-2-X
Library of Congress Catalog Card Number: 2001118542

Printed in the United States of America
Evangel Press
Nappanee, Indiana

Our acknowledgement and thanks to the NASA space program for the remarkable photographs of our universe and solar system that helped in the design of this book cover. Through the efforts of NASA we are privileged to enjoy a more intimate glimpse into God's remarkable creation.

Contents

Chapter 1   Introduction
Which God Are We Talking About?

Page 1

Chapter 2   God's First Revelation
Of Himself To The Human Family

Page 16

Chapter 3   God's Second Revelation
Of Himself To The Human Family

Page 37

Chapter 4   God's Third Revelation
Of Himself To The Human Family

Page 63

Chapter 5   God's Fourth Revelation
Of Himself To The Human Family

Page 85

Chapter 6   God's Fifth Revelation
Of Himself To The Human Family

Page 97

Chapter 7   God's Makeup and Characteristics

Page 109

Contents, Continued Next Page

Chapter 8   Why Does God Allow Bad Things To Happen
                  To His Human Creation?

                                               Page 137

Chapter 9   Does God Really Get Involved With
                  Individual Lives or Are We Left Alone
                  To Fight Our Battles By Ourselves?

                                               Page 149

Chapter 10   Ready For Some More Really Good News?

                                               Page 164

Author's Biography   Page 190

Other Titles In This Series   Page 193

Bibliography   Page 196

Introduction   *Chapter One*

Introduction
Which God Are We Talking About?

Hi, I'm Ken Howard

You and I are family. We may not have the same last name or come from the same country, but we're still family. We live together on this planet called earth and someday soon we'll venture on to another life. That fact alone makes us family...and puts us on the same common ground.

You and I also have questions that we want answered... but we want the real facts and truth. The problem is...there are a lot of conflicting philosophies floating around out there that could make a person wonder if there is any real truth to be found anywhere. But that's not a problem, as you will soon learn.

This is your life and my life we're dealing with here, and we want to make sure that we have the correct information so that you and I can make the best decisions for our life as we possibly can.

That's why this little book was written. It was written for you...just because you're worth the effort. I hope you will find it helpful in your pursuit toward enjoying the very best that life has to offer. The good thing about life is...life can be a good thing. Enjoy!

Introduction　　　　　　　　　　　　　　　　　　　**Chapter One**

WHO CAN YOU TRUST
TO REALLY TELL YOU THE TRUTH?

You're going to appreciate what you learn from these next few chapters. They help to answer some of the questions about God that many people seem to be confused about.

No, I don't claim to be the expert on God. Frankly, I don't know anyone who is. I'm just a person like yourself, seeking to separate reality from myth…and I've been privileged to have access to some of the most brilliant minds and research on the planet. You are the recipient of the most up-to-date and thorough information available on the topic of God.

I've been a student and teacher on the topic of life for more years than I wish to admit…and in those years I've learned that there is no question that cannot be answered and no problem that cannot be solved…including knowing who God is.

The two primary questions we will answer in this writing are…"Do we know for certain that a God does exist?" and… "Can God be trusted, since it appears He allows evil, pain and suffering to continue in our world…even on the innocent?"

This writing is not intended as an endorsement for any humanly organized religion or religious group, nor is there an agenda to convert you to some religion. It's my understanding that "religion" and "spirituality" are different things…and that you don't have to be religious to become acquainted with God.

2

Introduction   ***Chapter One***

There are some things about God that we human beings know to be true from scientific discoveries, history, human experiences and common sense. God really isn't all that confusing when we separate the facts from the myth. And that's precisely where this writing is headed...because you and I are worth the effort of knowing the truth.

It is with these thoughts in mind that I share some of the things man has discovered to be true about God.

DOES IT MATTER WHETHER OR NOT
WE BELIEVE AND TRUST IN GOD?

Consider this...if there is no God then we simply live and die and that's it. But if there is a God...then there is a higher authority in the universe to who we are subserviently responsible...and by who we may be judged in the next life.

IS IT POSSIBLE TO
SORT OUT THE CONFUSION?

It's natural for a person to be curious about God. Sometime in our life's journey the topic of God becomes an important priority. It's a topic we all want to get resolved...and apparently, we have only one opportunity to do so. Naturally, we want to be sure that we have the correct information.

Introduction   **Chapter One**

Our human ancestors haven't made it very easy for us, however. Over the centuries they've invented some pretty strange "god's" as objects of worship. It seems that someone at sometime or another has worshiped everything from insects and reptiles to celestial stars...not to mention that we humans have also tried to elevate ourselves to godly status...to worship self.

Then there are the present-day religions with their conflicting messages, which doesn't make it any easier for us to sort out the real truth. Each religion declares itself to be the representative of the one God...but how can everyone be right?

It also doesn't help to be living in the age of "intellectual enlightenment" where New Age philosophies blitz us with suggestions that there may not even be a God after all ...that everything around us happened pot luck...and we're pretty much on our own.

Adding to the confusion is all the bad stuff that's happening...evil, crime, disease, natural disasters, birth defects, death, etc., etc. The question on a lot of minds is, "If God does exist, why is there so much pain and suffering on planet earth?

So, the big question on many minds is ..."Can a person really sort out truth and reality in the midst of all the confusion?

The good news, fortunately, is yes. By laying aside personal prejudice, looking at the evidence, and applying some common sense...you and I can know the real truth...even in the midst of chaos. It's just a matter of personal sincerity.

Introduction   ***Chapter One***

BEING SKEPTICAL ISN'T A BAD THING

It's a normal and wise thing to be skeptical, especially when we are looking for truth on such an important topic.

The truth about any subject is only as good as the source of information. This is especially true on the topic we are dealing with here...for there is a great deal of speculation, false science and bad theology bouncing around out there regarding the subject of God.

Somewhere between religious dogmatism, ancient superstitions and New Age ideology there exists reality and truth where you and I can understand the fullness of who God is and how God relates to our human family. That's where this writing is headed...to explore that reality and truth.

But how do you know that what you are about to read is the truth? You'll know, because it makes sense...it computes with reality. Besides, it's all confirmed by historical facts and every scientific discovery known to modern man. We've done our homework!

WHICH GOD ARE WE TALKING ABOUT?

Before we look at the question, "Does any God really exist?", we first must identify which God possibly could exist...for there is a lot of differing opinions about a Deity.

5

Introduction   ***Chapter One***

Philosophers, scholars, theologians, religionists, humanists, agnostics and atheists all take their stab at defining God…some rather complimentary and some not so complimentary. So, who do we believe and how can we know for sure which God should be taken seriously?

That answer will become evident in a moment, but first, without getting too "philosophical" or "theological" in this discussion, let's take a brief look at how different people (religions) view "God"…or…a "Divine Presence".

THE GOD
OF
THE ATHEIST

The atheist God is known as *"Bagatelle"*. But, wait a minute, the atheist doesn't believe in God! Sure they do…they just don't believe in the real God.

Worshippers of *Bagatelle* include those involved with Secular Humanism, Marxism and Confucianism.

Their God, *Bagatelle*, has created everything you see around you. He is responsible for the perfect harmony and precise science that keeps the entire universe in motion.

Bagatelle created life. Bagatelle controls and maintains all existing matter and life forms. Bagatelle can do everything humans can't do…the greatest miracle worker known to man.

6

| _Introduction_ | _Chapter One_ |

"Bagatelle" means "nothing", and...according to atheistic logic, "nothing" created and maintains everything you see in existence...where everything is in perfect order.

Something from "Nothing" is the greatest miracle ever known to mankind. Science still doesn't believe it can happen.

The problem with the atheistic god is...it's all just human speculation. The atheist provides no scientific evidence to prove the non-existence of a real God. Forget the "science" of evolution, which has been a disaster to atheistic argument.

I think I will pass on the humanistic logic of atheism, avoiding the seduction of _Bagatelle's_ believers who continue to give reverence and worship to _Nothing_ as their god.

THE REVIVED ANCIENT GODS OF
NEW AGE PHILOSOPHERS

Closely related to "Bagatelle" are those "monistic" religions such as Hinduism, Buddhism, Sikhism, Sufism and the New Age Movement, who believe in an "Impersonal Oneness".

I've studied these religions for years, but I still don't get it. Honestly speaking, monism is just another example of "philosophical gobbledygook" that takes you nowhere.

Their concept of a human being is that "we are caught in the illusion of separateness, but we are identical in essence to the oneness"...whatever that means.

Introduction   *Chapter One*

Our basic human problem, according to monism, is that we are ignorant of our innate divinity...so the solution is "enlightenment"...i.e., to "realize our essence as the same as the oneness"...whatever that means.

Your reward when you become enlightened? You get reincarnated to live on this earth...with all its problems, pain and suffering for another lifetime...or, you get to merge into the impersonal oneness... whatever that means.

I think I'll pass on this one too.

THE YIN YANG GOD

Then there are the views of Taoism, known as the "yin/yang" or "*balancing dualism*" philosophy...that defines God as "two opposing, but interacting and balancing forces".

According to this belief, we humans are a microcosm of the two interacting forces...and our problem is...we are living out of alignment with nature. The solution? Live in harmony (alignment) with nature...whatever that means.

Your reward for doing so? Maybe you will advance to some form in the spirit world. Then, maybe not...for who knows for sure?

If a person is looking for real hope, maybe he or she should "yin" or "yang" out of here...and look elsewhere.

Introduction   **Chapter One**

POLYTHEISM

The "polytheistic" view is that there are many Gods, not just one. Worshippers of many Gods are usually found in the "tribal" or "folk" religions, such as Voodoo and Shinto. Major world religions do not accept more than one God.

In polytheism, man's problem is defined as "angering the gods". Thus, man's total and ceaseless pursuit in worship is to appease the gods with the hope that "sometimes the person advances to the spirit world".

THE YIN
WITHOUT THE YANG
GOD

The religion of Zoroastrianism teaches a *"Competing Dualism"*, which is similar to *Balancing Dualism* (YIN/YANG) in that both believe in the existence of two opposing gods. But in *competing dualism* these two opposing gods are not interacting or balancing forces...one is good and one is evil. This is not a God-devil battle where God is more powerful.

In this religion man was created to join the good god in the battle against evil. Man's problem is when he chooses to do evil. The solution? ... Choose to do good. Zoroastrianism also teaches rewards and punishments in either heaven or hell.

Introduction   **Chapter One**

MONOTHEISM

Monotheism, as taught by the world's three largest religions (Christianity, Judaism, Islam), is a belief in the existence of one transcendent and supreme God, who is the Creator of all things. These religions also teach that human beings are a distinct and separate creation from all animals.

While the teachings of Judaism, Christianity and Islam may have similar overtones...they are all remarkably different. The problem of mankind, according to Islamic teaching, is failing to seek God's guidance. Judaism sees man's problem as breaking God's laws, while the Christian belief identifies mankind as rebellious toward God.

In another writing entitled, "True Meaningful Religion" we do an in-depth study into the beginning, founders and teachings of these three largest world religions...and others.

THE GODS OF THE NEW AGE...
SECULAR HUMANISM PHILOSOPY

The modern day religions known as the "New Age Movement" and "Secular Humanism" are just outgrowths of some of the ancient Eastern religions, floating between atheistic and monistic philosophies. They really offer nothing new...just a new spin on how to define "man as his own boss (god)".

Introduction   *Chapter One*

SO, WHERE DOES ALL THIS DIVERSITY
OF A GOD CONCEPT
LEAVE US?

Actually it is very encouraging...for we know that for something to be absolute truth...something else must be false.

This is quite evident in mankind's quest for "god"... where various "religious" and "philosophical" concepts have emerged without any basis or proof of credibility. The challenge in all this confusion is to find the real truth about God that has been proven to be credible.

Different "religions" and "religious concepts" make it very annoying in pursuing the truth about God...but by no means, impossible. With so many different religious beliefs and philosophical myths being promoted, there is hardly any space to take a deep breath to figure out which, if any, "religious teaching " has credibility. But we can...and will.

Let's assume that there is only one God in the universe, which is what the major religions teach. If that be the case, then it would stand to reason that one God would define only one religion as His ambassador on earth to reveal His one truth about Himself.

Forget the argument that different cultures and tongues require a different message and religion. That doesn't make sense.

11

Introduction   *Chapter One*

A true God would know how to teach one message to different skin colors and to people who talk differently than you and I do. Common sense would suggest that, what God expects from one culture, He expects from all cultures.

Simple logic would reject the idea that one God would develop different religions and religious teachings in an effort to reveal Himself and His will for the human race. Such a plan would be hazardous to consistency and unity of God's message. Religious confusion is not God's answer for mankind.

If this logic is reasonable, then we must assume that there are true religious teachings in the world and there are false religious teachings...and that there is only one way to know God. But how does a person distinguish between true and false religious teaching? The answer is ... credibility.

True religion and its teachings can be proven by historical, scientific, moral and judicious scrutiny. False religion cannot. False religion has flaws and errors. Is there a teaching about God that has a proven credibility? Absolutely!

CURRENT WORLD RELIGIONS

There are eleven major active religions in the world and numerous other "religious philosophies"...not to mention a zillion or so cults that have been dreamed up by some guy on a boring Sunday afternoon.

12

Introduction   _Chapter One_

The four largest religions are Buddhism, Islam, Judaism and Christianity (Christianity being the largest)...each having a concept of a Supreme Being with differing personalities.

Buddhism has a historically confusing and changing belief of a Deity with the current worship being directed toward Gautama (Buddha), the modern founder of modern Buddhism.

Islam, or Mohammedism, identifies one God named Allah, yet places Mohammed, the founder of Islam, on a level of Deity who is also worthy of worship. Mohammedism was created as an alternative religion to Judaism and Christianity.

Judaism identifies Jehovah as one Supreme Being and Creator of the Universe. It also declares that the Jewish people are God's chosen people with special privileges from God.

Christianity defines God as one Supreme Being who has revealed Himself in three persons (Trinity) as God the Father (Jehovah), God the Son (Jesus) and God the Holy Spirit.

Although modern Christianity has become divided in its organizational structure, methods of worship and theology...the unified message is still centered around Jesus as being the promised Messiah (Christ) for all mankind...as predicted by the Jewish prophets of the Old Testament.

The fundamental belief of Christianity is that Jesus was God in the flesh, who came to earth to reveal God and to redeem mankind from their rebellion against God.

Introduction   **Chapter One**

OTHER GOD CONCEPTS

There are also "philosophical" views of a deity that are not associated with a precise Being. Among these modern views are Deism, Pantheism, Panentheism, Finite Godism and Polytheism. The credibility for these views appears only to be in the logic of the person who proposed the theory.

With that all said, let's turn our attention back to God... with a brief review of what we have concluded so far.

First ... based on all the evidence from science, history and human experience...the conclusion is...that if there is a God, there is only one God who is the Creator of the natural universe, as we know it.

Second ... we acknowledge the fact that there are false religions and false religious teachings that are rooted in human philosophy and human ambition...rather than in the truth of Divine revelation.

Third ... in our search for truth, it is <u>not</u> necessary that we explain or justify false beliefs or false teachers. They have the onus on themselves of providing proof for their teaching... rather than demanding that we provide proof for their error.

Fourth ... truth is available and can be understood by all people. True religious teaching can be confirmed by scientific scrutiny, historical reality and moral integrity. Is there such a religious teaching? The answer is yes...without doubt!

Introduction   ***Chapter One***

Ok, that's the introduction to the topic of God. It simply says that there are a lot of foolish ideas floating around that have no affect on our search for truth. Knowing the real God is not an impossible task, or even an overwhelming challenge.

You and I can know the real God, and we can be assured that what we know is not clouded with superstition or error. That's the good news. The bad news is, too many people don't take it seriously enough to pursue a personal investigation of their Creator...but allow false teachers to lead them down a blind alley to a miserable life.

With that little sermon said, let's now pursue our quest of understanding who the real God is...and how this real God relates to our human family.

The place to begin is to look at the "Five Miraculous Events" where God has revealed Himself to our human family.

These events have been confirmed by scientific scrutiny and historical accuracy as being beyond question.

There is no doubt ... God does exist. Everywhere we look, reality just keeps getting better and better.

15

The Universe, God's Revelation   *Chapter Two*

God's First Revelation
Of Himself
To Our Human Family...

The Physical Universe

YES...SCIENCE HAS DEFINITELY PROVEN
THE EXISTENCE OF GOD

A miraculous event has taken place. There is a universe around us that is so complex, so meticulously balanced and so perfectly harmonized, from the largest galaxy to the smallest sub-atomic particle, that it'll blow your hat off when it all really sinks in. Someone must have designed it and Someone must be maintaining it all, since it all functions in such perfect harmony.

Every time I look into a sunset or read about the carbon exchange in an atom, it's as though I'm reading a postcard with the words... "Greetings and best wishes. I hope you enjoy my gift of creation that I made just for you." Signed, God

The Universe, God's Revelation   *Chapter Two*

I've always wondered how anyone could look at the remarkable precision of life and ever doubt that a Divine Creator with a Divine plan was involved...yet they still try.

The most knowledgeable Physicists and Astronomers on the earth share their observations of a universe so complex, so precise and so immense that it demands attention to the question, "How did it all happen? Every time they look into a test tube or telescope, their hearts must pound with awe.

But let me be honest...using the argument of the universe as evidence to God's existence brings a snicker and a scoff from those who worship *"Bagatelle"*. The atheist is well aware that the universe is real and that it makes a very powerful statement that something or Someone caused its existence.

This is where the atheist has tried to put his best foot forward...to replace the real God with his god, "Bagatelle". The atheist says that "Bagatelle" (nothing) created the universe... that all this stuff we see floating in space just happened by itself without any prior design or planning. Wow! What a miracle that would be ... that nothing could become something so complex as the universe ... and that the entire universe all works in perfect harmony without anybody telling it to. Miraculous!

I wonder if you could build a house or make a ballpoint pen that way...from nothing? Bagatelle, if you do exist, I applaud you ... but my scientific research friends tell me, that when it comes to creating something ... "nothing" didn't do it.

17

The Universe, God's Revelation　　　　　　　　　　*Chapter Two*

There is a pointed debate going on between "evolutionists" and "creationists" that flood the hard copy media with their arguments. Books, articles and web sites (seemingly by the millions) are devoted to the "scientific" evidence on both sides of how all things came into existence.

This argument between evolutionists and creationists will never go away...even as the evidence continues to pile up in favor of a designed universe. In another writing, entitled "Your Life And Beyond", we look more deeply into the pros and cons of both opinions... to give "Bagatelle" his day on the witness stand.

In all the literature I've read, it appears that the atheistic approach to the discussion is to ridicule...rather than to present evidence. Rather than presenting logical and proven facts, it seems that the atheist prefers to denounce all those who disagree with them...as ignorant or as religious dogmatists.

I disagree with that position, for I know many highly educated scientists who have confirmed, through extensive research, that the universe and human life are creations of God.

The universe where all the parts function in perfect harmony with one another is not in dispute. Everybody agrees... everything has a unique position and purpose to the whole.

There can be only one of three alternatives to the question, "How did it all come together with such perfect precision?"

18

The Universe, God's Revelation   **Chapter Two**

ONE... The universe has always existed, will always exist and is self-maintaining (steady state theory)

TWO... The universe is self-born, self-correcting and self- maintained by random chance (evolution theory)

THREE... The universe is a Divine design and creation of God, Who provides continual maintenance (creation doctrine)

Before we review the arguments of those alternatives, let's take a brief journey back to our freshman science class to put this all in perspective. While this writing is not intended to be a scientific essay, there are some insights from science that remind us of how remarkably fine tuned everything operates in relationship to the whole, to ask an honest question...

"Could the universe have actually evolved on its own, or must there have been a designer and creator who put all the pieces together in perfect harmony with everything?"

A BRIEF LOOK AT THE UNIVERSE

The more that astronomers investigate, the more we learn how vast, precise and perfect all the elements of the universe are in their relationship with one another. There exists within the universe a uniqueness of time, space, light, matter, position, interaction and subsistence that is amazing, to say the least. There is no argument from "eternalists", "evolutionists" or "creationists" on this issue.

The Universe, God's Revelation   **Chapter Two**

Some suggestions measure the universe between ten and twenty billion light-years across, although scientists have yet to locate the center. Beyond the Milky Way galaxy in which we live there are at least a hundred billion other galaxies, each of which contains about one hundred billion stars.

GALAXIES

The galaxies spread unevenly across the vast universe. In some areas the galaxies cluster together while in other areas of the universe there are regions known as "Great Voids" where few galaxies exist.

In 1989 a discovery was made of the largest structure in the universe, which scientists call "The Great Wall"...so named because of the huge concentration of clustered galaxies.

Another region just recently discovered is referred to as "The Great Attractor". This area is so large that it is attracting other regions toward it, including the Milky Way and our "Local Group" cluster of other galaxies, all of which are speeding toward The Great Attractor at one million miles per hour.

Galactic clusters create a problem with the "old universe" theory. Studies of galactic clusters reveal a lack of enough gravitational force to hold them together very long. There isn't enough mass in the clusters to overcome the velocities at which the galaxies are moving.

The Universe, God's Revelation   **Chapter Two**

What this means is…the clusters could not have existed for billions of years as some theories suggest. They would have long ago become extinct.

STARS

The centerpieces of our heaven appear to be the stars. While the exact number of stars in the universe is unknown, the number that is suggested is somewhere between 10^{20} and 10^{24} (10 followed by 24 zeroes). With the naked eye we can only see a small fraction of the stars just in our own galaxy.

Stars vary in size; some smaller than our moon and others with diameters exceeding one billion miles…yet there remains enormous distances between the stars to insure against accidental collision. For example, our closest neighboring sun (Alpha Centauri) is 4.3 light-years away.

Stars continually create gigantic hydrogen explosions that generate light and heat. At the core, some stars generate as much as 40 million degrees centigrade. It is from these stars that our world enjoys beauty of the night and needed warmth.

PLANETS

Circling our sun in an orderly manner is an assortment of planets, moons, asteroids and dust.

21

The Universe, God's Revelation   **Chapter Two**

Among those is Venus, which is much like the earth in size, mass and density…yet life could not exist there because of other variables. Venus' rotation cycle is almost eight months in a reverse direction of the other planets. Its atmospheric pressure is ninety times that of earth with a surface temperature of about 1,000 degrees Fahrenheit. Hurricane winds, repeated lightening strikes and deafening thunder add to the impossibility of life.

Similar limitations hold true of other neighboring planets … Mars, Jupiter and Saturn.

The earth, on the other hand, is friendly to life. For example, the earth's magnetic field protects us from the sun's dangerous radiation (other planets do not have such a magnetic field).

Our moon also provides help for life to exist on earth by keeping the earth from rotating three times faster than it does (which would subject us to continuous gale force winds). The moon also protects the earth's axis from Jupiter's gravitational pull.

Scientists agree that our hospitable planet (earth) is a _precise_ collection of _all_ the correct elements and circumstances to support human life.

The evolutionist theory tries to suggest that this perfect order of things has evolved over time by mere chance…but most scientists have concluded that such precision cannot be explained as occurring by mere coincidence.

22

The Universe, God's Revelation   **Chapter Two**

SUN

The earth's personal star, which we refer to as the "sun", is also quite remarkable. As stars go, the sun is not very large and not particularly hot...yet it provides an almost inexhaustible supply of energy necessary for human life on earth.

The sun's core temperature is fifteen million degrees centigrade, converting five million tons of mass energy every second to the adjacent universe. The earth intercepts only one billionth of this solar energy, which is all we need for our survival. The sun gives off more energy in one second than all the people on earth have produced in the entire history of the world.

Ninety percent of all earth's useable energy comes from the sun. The sun's nuclear fusion reaction is released in the form of "photons" that take 8 minutes to reach the earth's surface. Trillions of these photons hit each square meter of earth's surface every second.

The sun is at the _exact distance_ from the earth for life on earth to survive. If the sun were one mile closer or one mile farther away, the earth would be too hot or too cold for survival.

The sun's axis is at a _precise_ 15 degrees from the earth's axis to maintain the earth's rotational balance. A change of one degree axis would melt the polar ice and unbalance the earth, causing a rabid erratic rotation where life would be impossible.

23

The Universe, God's Revelation   **Chapter Two**

Again, the question, "Could this perfect precision have happened merely by chance or must we consider a Divine Designer and Creator?"

OTHER SPACE PHENOMENA

The universe is a complex engineering design that astounds those who review its intricacy. Beyond the perfect placement of planets and earths to their suns, there are other relationships involving Black Holes, Neutron Stars, Pulsars, Magnetars, Gamma Ray Bursts, Supernovas, Quasars, Nebulae, Comets, Asteroids, Meteoroids and Cosmic Dust.

Neutron stars are the smallest in the universe, typically measuring only about ten miles in diameter. Yet, amazingly, the mass of a neutron star is so dense that a thimbleful would weigh one hundred million tons.

Pulsars are rapidly spinning neutron stars that emit "pulses" of radio waves. Normal stars rotate about once a month while pulsars can rotate as fast as 100 times a second.

Magnetars spin even faster (200 times per second) and have magnetic fields 100 times larger than the neutron stars, which is a trillion times larger than our sun's magnetic field.

Gamma ray random bursts are the most energetic form of electromagnetic radiation known in the universe. They are several thousand times more powerful than visible light and

24

| The Universe, God's Revelation | Chapter Two |

have at times been identified to be as bright as all the stars in the universe combined. These random "flashes" of intense high-energy radiation can release ten thousand times the energy that our sun will produce over its entire lifetime.

Supernovas are massive explosions that destroy an entire star, emitting light in excess of a billion times the normal level. This striking increase of illumination can last several weeks before fading.

Quasars are extremely radiant at all wavelengths. They can be a thousand times brighter than entire galaxies, even though the galaxy may be hundreds of thousands times larger.

Nebulae are clouds of dust particles and gas, often containing enough material to form a hundred thousand stars.

Comets are small bodies with eccentric elliptical orbits. On their approach swing around the sun, frozen materials vaporize to form a long tail of gas and dust.

Asteroids are small planet-like bodies, some as large as 600 miles in diameter while others as small as a stone. Most orbit in the asteroid belt between Mars and Jupiter, yet some have orbital paths that cross the Earth's orbit.

Meteoroids are small asteroids in the solar system. Some are on a collision course with Earth. Most are tiny and burn up in the Earth's atmosphere (Meteors, Shooting Stars). Others survive to strike the Earth (Meteorites). Ten thousand tons of Cosmic dust strikes the Earth's atmosphere each year.

The Universe, God's Revelation   **Chapter Two**

TIME, SPACE, LIGHT

Light is something we take for granted, yet it is a metaphysical event that is quite extraordinary. The speed of light has been calculated to be 186,000 miles per second. This speed remains constant regardless of circumstance or frame of reference. Nothing in the known universe can exceed the speed of light. At the speed of light, time stops.

Light flows in packets of energy called "photons". Every second, one trillion photons from the sun's energy source falls on each pinhead-sized area of earth. These photons are amazingly small. For example, a 100 watt light bulb discharges about 200 million trillion (2×10^{20}) photons each second.

The retina of the human eye contains over 127 million photoreceptor cells known as rods and cones. These cells are light sensitive, converting images into electrical signals that can be interpreted by the brain. As few as one or two photons of light can cause a visual signal in each rod.

Photons never age, the reason being...time stops at the speed of light. A photon released from a far away star several thousands of years ago hasn't aged one second. When we look into the sky to see a bright star, we are looking thousands of years into the past. The star may have exploded thousands of years ago, yet the photons traveling at 186,000 miles per second have had a long distance to travel to reach our eye.

26

The Universe, God's Revelation   **Chapter Two**

Time moves only in one direction. It moves forward, and at the same pace for all people. We all share equally in this one resource. But when we reach out of our earthly environment into the vast universe, the law of time changes and time warps dramatically.

Einstein's relativity redefined what was originally thought of time, space and light. He explained light to be a discrete quantum (photon) that travels at the same speed for all frames of reference regardless of circumstance. Also, when something accelerates to the speed of light, both space and time react eccentrically.

In other words...Einstein's formula identifies that, at the speed of light..."dimension shrinks to zero, mass increases to infinity and time stands still".

THE MESSAGE IN ALL THIS...?

The dimensions and precision of all this time, space and light demands a common sense conclusion...which is...things just do not come together the way they are without some kind of a plan. This brings us back to the only logical answer...God had to have created it all. Nothing else makes sense.

The more mankind delves into the complexities of the universe...it's easy to understand why most world scientists believe in God.

27

The Universe, God's Revelation   **Chapter Two**

A BRIEF LOOK
AT
THE INVISIBLE WORLD

The science of Physics is concerned with the interaction of energy, force and matter...while the science of Chemistry is involved with the composition, structure and properties of substances. Both sciences reveal an invisible world so infinitesimally small and energetic that it has boggled the mind of every scientist who ventures to explore it.

Take atoms for example. Atoms form the basic units of chemical elements and are some of the smallest units of matter...although not the smallest. To comprehend how small an atom is, consider this analogy...an atom would compare in size to an apple as an apple would compare in size to the entire earth.

Modern science has discovered even smaller elements than atoms. There are ninety-two naturally occurring chemical elements. Eighty-one are stable and eleven are radioactive...to transform themselves into other elements over time. Particle accelerators further identify an additional 20 elements, some with a life span lasting only one hundred thousandth of a second.

Carbon is the major element with distinguishing characteristics to support life, and is found in all life forms on earth.

The Universe, God's Revelation   **Chapter Two**

The combining of two smaller elements is what forms carbon, which in itself is a remarkable miracle when we consider an element's short life span and the intricate process of the elements bonding with one another in such a short life span.

For example, the life span of some elements is only 10^{-16} seconds ($100,000,000,000,000,000^{th}$ of a second). Yet, during this infinitesimal time frame, two separate elements must bond together with a precise mathematical process to form carbon.

And, get this...even with all the different and special properties and elements that can bond together as two...to create carbon... every carbon in the universe is identical.

Human life would not exist without the perfectly matched energy stimulation of these elements. The bonding of two elements...to create carbon for human life...is so mathematically precise, so exact, and so rapid...that it defies any human explanation of how it could occur.

But, that's not all. There are also other atomic elements essential to life...oxygen, hydrogen, chloride, potassium, phosphorus, iron, calcium, sodium, and nitrogen. And each of these tiny elements has a specific role in the process of life.

The question is, "Could such intricacy and exactness be the result of coincidence through evolution or must we consider a Divine Creator with a Divine design?" The answer is rather obvious to satisfy the criteria for pure science. "Bagatelle" could not have produced something so precise and perfect.

29

The Universe, God's Revelation   **Chapter Two**

Only God, with a plan, could have designed and perfected it all. Only a Divine blueprint could organize such intricacy in such a limited amount of time.

THE HUMAN BODY

We will not take the space in this writing to look at the amazing complexity of the human body. The body's uniqueness and perfection of design is so elaborate that it alone demands an answer ... "Could any perfectly operating system such as the human body be the result of mere chance or coincidence?" Could fish dung from the ocean's floor have actually become YOU? Surely, we humans are more unique than that. I refer you to the writing entitled, "Your Life And Beyond".

Evolution is an abysmal scientific speculation without empirical justification. It cannot explain the perfect order of the vast universe as being the product of mere chance. No pure logic could accept the "something from nothing" concept...nor can we accept the rationale that "a human heart, mind, soul and body evolved from non-living fish dung".

As we consider the complexity, vastness and precision of the universe...and all things therein...we cannot but be amazed with its design. With all the publicity about "evolution", most people are not aware that the majority of scientists on the planet accept the reality of a Divine Creator.

The Universe, God's Revelation   **Chapter Two**

It is virtually impossible for true science to accept the phenomena of time, space, mass, light and energy to have developed so complex and perfectly by mere coincidence of evolution. Nor can science justify the biological and chemical complexities within the invisible elements of all life to be anything other than by design.

Scientific logic submits to an engineered creation by design...yet there are a few scientific philosophers who theorize another origin of life in an attempt to refute the existence or authority of our Creator.

THEORIES OF ORIGIN

From the middle of the nineteenth century there have been questions and debates within the scientific community regarding the origin of the universe and all life forms therein. The debate centers on whether or not there is a Divine Being (God) who created all things, or whether the universe and life forms are self-existent through an evolutionary process.

A great amount of media attention (supposedly impartial) has created confusion in many minds as to the reality of what science actually knows about the origin of things. Does science really know how the universe came into being? Have the results of scientific discovery been improperly reported?

31

The Universe, God's Revelation   *Chapter Two*

Yes, true science knows that the universe did not evolve over a long period of time in opposition to the popular "evolutionist" theory. Yes, the findings of true science are being distorted and withheld by the mass media...who take pleasure in promoting the false theory of evolution. More sadly, our public education system teaches evolution as a scientific fact when, in reality, it has never been so proven.

In fact, the more that science learns, the more evolution is discredited. The current trend of most scientists is to accept the creation principle as certain. Let's look at some of the data regarding the theories of origin ...

THE INFINITE, PERPETUAL
STEADY STATE THEORY

The simplistic suggestion from this theory is that the universe and all life forms have always existed...without beginning or end. This theory comes from philosophical speculation without any scientific support.

Scientific evidence totally refutes this suggestion, knowing in fact that the universe had a beginning and is gradually coming to an end. Additionally, evidence now confirms the universe to have been created in an instant moment of time...referred to by some scientists as "The Big Bang".

32

THE SELF-FORMED
EVOLUTION THEORY

From around the time of Aristotle through the middle of the nineteenth century, a new philosophy regarding *spontaneous generation* was strongly promoted.

Prior to that time there was no problem about the origin of life, even though it was known that life spontaneously arose from non-living things, i.e. maggots from decaying meat, frogs from stagnant ponds, earthworms from manure, etc.

Scientific experiments later proved that decaying meat, stagnant ponds and manure only served as "nests" in which living eggs were deposited. Nevertheless, spontaneous generation was not to go away quietly.

A Dutch scientist discovered the world of bacteria that further research proved was everywhere, and which appeared to support the spontaneous generation theory. In later research, culminating with those of Louis Pasteur, it was proven that bacteria reside in the air, which can produce bacteria in decomposing non-life substance.

Yet, the old adage that "people will believe what they wish to believe regardless of evidence", was proved to be true in some minds, even though most scientists refuted the "spontaneous generation theory".

The Universe, God's Revelation   **Chapter Two**

When the "spontaneous generation" logic was shattered through scientific studies, it became a problem for the few philosophers who did not want to accept the origin of life as being a creation of God. They were now challenged to find alternative solutions.

In 1859 Charles Darwin published his work entitled "The Origin of Species" and later a Russian biochemist (A.I. Oparin) proposed a theory of the chemical origin of life. From these two non-proven theories arose the "materialistic" view that justified the "mechanistic" view of evolution. The mechanistic view relied on pure chance for the development of all things, while the materialistic view suggests that evolution is predestined when the conditions are right and when there is enough time to accomplish the process. In other words, given enough time anything is possible...according to "materialistic evolution". That theory caught hold in many minds without any scientific support.

Currently, materialistic evolution is being taught in all levels of education as scientific fact. This is unfortunate, since no area of science has been able to prove the theory of evolution as having any basis of credibility. In fact, the more that scientific research continues, the more it proves the fallacy of the evolution suggestion. True science has challenged the evolution theory at every point to refute the possibility of chance evolution and to confirm creation.

The Universe, God's Revelation   *Chapter Two*

So why do so many believe and teach evolution? The only obvious answer is...evolution is an attempt by those who wish to deny the existence of a Creator...regardless of the true evidence. To real science, this is astonishing, to say the least.

THE "DIVINE CREATION" POSSIBILITY

The ancient Greeks viewed science as a philosophical issue. Their method of science was to reason things out rather than performing experiments. To them, the world was not created, thus unknowable.

It was not until a Theistic view of creation came along that science began to study the world experimentally. The thought that God had created all matter was the enticing motive for the beginning of scientific investigation. Identifying God as the Creator, who also is in complete control, helped scientists to make the assumption that the universe made sense.

Those who drafted the practice of modern science were "creationists". Modern science owes its foundation of investigative curiosity to those who explored the "unique and remarkable created universe".

A British astronomer observed, "I have always thought it curious that, while most scientists claim to eschew religion, it actually dominates their thoughts more than it does the clergy."

35

The Universe, God's Revelation　　　　　　　　**Chapter Two**

SUMMARY

It is beyond scientific justification or mathematical probability to consider that the elements of the universe could exist in the perfect order and relationship with one another by coincidence.

The only legitimate possibility for such precise physics, chemistry and biology is that all the elements exist and function by Divine design.

Most scholarly and highly regarded scientists in all fields of study around the world accept the reality of a Divine created universe...to speak out very forcibly against the unscientific theory of evolution. They believe in God, as I do, because of the billions and trillions of reasons all around us.

As a researcher I cannot avoid the remarkable and abundant evidence within an intricately balanced universe to be anything other than by design and supernatural creation.

The universe and all things therein is a very powerful statement that defies any explanation other than ...God did it all!

The universe is one of the five revelations of God to the human family that undoubtedly confirms that God does indeed exist.

If there were no God, there would be no universe. Everywhere we look ... reality just keeps smiling back!

36

The Bible, God's Revelation   *Chapter Three*

God's Second Revelation
Of Himself
To Our Human Family...

The Book We Call The Bible

WHAT SCIENCE AND HISTORY
REVEAL TO BE TRUE
ABOUT THIS AWESOME BOOK

A miraculous event has taken place. A book was written thousands of years ago that contains truth and wisdom for human life, so up-to-date and relevant, that it could have easily been written in this generation.

It is the all time, number one bestseller. Every area of science and scholarship refers to it for guidance...applauding it for its wisdom. We call it "The Bible". Never has there been a book written that compares with it...religious or otherwise.

The Bible, God's Revelation   *Chapter Three*

Some people ask, "Why should I trust an old outdated book like the Bible? Did men not write the Bible? What makes the Bible more important than any other religious or ancient book? These are fair questions.

Most ancient writings are fun to read (if that's your thing), but they have no relevance to human life as we experience it today. Their ability or authority to provide meaningful answers for today's world doesn't exist...with one exception...the Bible.

The Bible is the most widely referred to book in human history. It is the scripture for the largest and most influential "religion" (Christianity) in all of human history. It continues to be the road map to life for millions of people throughout the world, who trust it with unwavering loyalty. Scientists, historians, health professionals, scholars (even military leaders) constantly refer to it. Why? Why is the Bible so intriguing to the masses of people from every walk of life throughout the entire world?

When a person takes the time to investigate the Bible's history and teachings...to understand the full reality of the Bible, there remains no doubt that it is another way in which God has revealed Himself to our human family. Its teachings are so powerful and up-to-date that it could literally solve every human problem on planet earth ... if everyone followed it's timeless wisdom. It is truly a miracle book.

38

The Bible, God's Revelation   *Chapter Three*

A pursuit of truth is dependent upon the credibility of the source. A credible source of information assures us of truth while a false source is "sifting sand" on which truth escapes the seeker...only to be replaced by error. It is for this reason that true research must first define the credibility of its information.

In spiritual matters, the religious "sacred scriptures" must pass rigorous examination of origin and relevance in order to prove credibility. A declaration from a certain religion to endorse a writing as their "sacred scriptures" is not sufficient to researchers as proof that they represent a higher spiritual truth.

That's where the Bible comes in. Over centuries of heavy scrutiny, the Bible has passed all tests of credibility and relevance...standing alone above all other religious writings as a document where truth is represented. Let's explore the evidence.

THE UNIQUENESS OF THE BIBLE

The Bible is a book of supernatural origin and history, a book that cannot be explained by human philosophy. Throughout its pages we are introduced to the supernatural, which we must either accept as truth or reject as fiction.

The events and characters of the Bible are either an elaborate hoax to deceive the human race or they are the words of a Divine Creator who has spoken to us through them.

The Bible, God's Revelation   ***Chapter Three***

No other book has been attacked and challenged like the Bible. There have been many attempts throughout history to destroy or discredit it, but no one has yet been able to do so. The Bible has survived its critics and political enemies to become the one single authority for human existence. It is the most widely read piece of literature available to the human race … and the more that we advance in scientific knowledge the more the Bible is confirmed to be correct in every detail.

Even though the Bible was written thousands of years ago, it still sheds insights on human nature, on world problems, and on human suffering so timely that it could have just as easily been written in this generation. There simply is no greater wisdom to be found anywhere else.

The reason the Bible is such a permanent and relevant book is because it is more than just another work of human literature. It claims to be the word of God. As we will shortly learn, this claim is well supported…both by internal and external evidence. There is no question that the one true God of the universe is the author of the Bible, as well as its guardian and its endorser.

In another writing entitled, "The Book We Call The Bible", we thoroughly explore its origin, its teachings and the many scientific proofs that continue to shed light on its accuracy and historical credibility. All true scholars and researchers accept this book as God's miraculous revelation.

40

The Bible, God's Revelation　　　　　　　**Chapter Three**

BUT, WHAT IS THE BIBLE?

The Bible claims to be God's written revelation of His will for the human race. Although it is a collection of 66 different books that were written by 40 different human writers over a period of approximately 1600 years, the Bible confesses to be "Divinely inspired". In other words, the 40 human writers recorded only those words that God inspired them to write.

Thirty-nine of the sixty-six books comprise the Old Testament while twenty-seven books comprise the New Testament. These two testaments (covenants) are records of the two covenants that God has made with the human race. The Old Testament was written in the Hebrew language many centuries before the birth and life of Jesus. It contains events and prophecies long before Jesus was born. The New Testament was written in the Greek language after Jesus had lived on earth. It records the events of Jesus' life as well as His teachings.

Our current English Bibles have been translated from these two original languages, the Hebrew and Greek... protecting the original message. The original copies of the Hebrew and Greek manuscripts are still available for research, and although Bible scholars refer to them for more clarification in their studies, it is not necessary to the common reader of the scriptures to be a language scholar in order to understand God's will and guidance for their life.

The Bible, God's Revelation   ***Chapter Three***

Throughout its pages the Bible claims to be divinely given, a claim made by no other book. Its writers make statements such as "the word of the Lord came to me", or, "God said", or, "thus saith the Lord". By these statements the writers confess that they are mere scribes who recorded only what God had revealed to them.

The Bible is not dependent only upon the claims of the writers, however. It also is supported to be of divine inspiration by the unity and perfect harmony of their message as well.

Consider this...the 40 writers of the Bible, who lived over a period of 1600 years without any opportunity to corroborate with each other about what they were to write...all wrote the same exact message in perfect harmony and unity with one another.

This perfect harmony and unity of message is a strong statement that a Divine mind must be behind what these human writers recorded...for how could 40 different men living in different generations have put together such a book with the precise and accurate message that it contains?

Forty different writers recorded God's thoughts at different times during 1600 years...and every one of them wrote about the same theme, the same characters and the same outcome. The perfect harmony and the orderly detail of its teachings confirm the claims of its writers...that the word of the Lord came upon them.

The Bible, God's Revelation   *Chapter Three*

THE BIBLE'S RELEVANCE
AND
PERMANENCE

While the priority of its teachings is spiritual, the Bible is also the leading authority on other important matters of human life...including moral, social, family, psychological, and physical health issues.

In all matters of importance to our well being the Bible stands alone in its wisdom. No human writing has yet to compare with the insights and instruction recorded in its pages.

As to its relevance, time has not left its marks on the Bible, for the Bible retains a perennial wisdom that is applicable to all generations, including the one in which we now live. This is not the case, however, with the books of human origin. The wisdom of human writings grows old and loses value in a short period of time. An entire library of human writings changes in every generation. The Bible, however, remains the one book that survives as a permanent fixture in human education.

The Bible continues to intrigue the minds of those who seek for truth ... attracting new readers every year. The reason is simple...the Bible continues to relate to human circumstance and experience with a wisdom that never grows old. It contains wisdom shared from the Divine mind of God that is far above the wisdom of any human being. That's why people read it.

The Bible, God's Revelation   *Chapter Three*

The Bible meets the deeper needs of all people... regardless of age, race or circumstance. It is the only universal book capable of speaking to the needs of all people everywhere.

The Bible answers the deep questions that would otherwise be hidden. It explains who we are, why we exist and where we are headed. It reveals how man can regain fellowship with God and provides a hope that there is an eternal life beyond this present world.

Only in the Bible can we find the fulfillment for all our needs and solutions to all our problems ... something that no mere human writing is capable of doing. That alone gives credence to its Divine Author.

THE BIBLE'S CENTRAL CHARACTER

The Bible identifies a central figure that human writers could not create. It reveals the person of Jesus Christ, who outmatches all heroes and fictional characters invented by men.

Both the Old and New Testament writers describe Jesus with all the attributes of a Divine God. The writers of the Old Testament were inspired of God to prophesy the coming of Jesus, while the New Testament writers became the biographers and eyewitnesses of His earthly visit. Both revealed the same Divine person who fulfilled every prophecy that had been spoken of Him hundreds of years before He was born.

The Bible, God's Revelation   *Chapter Three*

The Old Testament prophets could not have known about a virgin birth or where Jesus would be born, or the date He would be born, or about the many events surrounding His life...yet they described those events in precise detail hundreds of years before they happened.

In fact, the Old Testament writers recorded 300 different prophecies regarding every aspect of the life of Jesus... including His trial, crucifixion, and resurrection from the dead.

There can be only one conclusion to their prophetic ability...the Old Testament writers wrote by the inspiration of the Divine mind of God, who told them exactly what to write.

But the prophesies of future events do not end with the life of Jesus. The Bible, whose writing was completed around 95 A.D., contains precise prophesies of political and religious events that have taken place throughout history, from the date of Jesus' death and resurrection in the year 33 A.D., up to and including things that have happened in our current generation.

The ability of the Bible to see into the future with such remarkable detail and accuracy is a powerful support that it is more than just a collection of human writings.

THE BIBLE'S
"SUPERNATURAL" REVELATIONS

45

The Bible, God's Revelation   *Chapter Three*

The Bible records events that man has never witnessed or that science cannot explain beyond what the Bible teaches.

The Biblical account of creation is a simple and satisfactory explanation to the beginning of all things. It tells from where the universe and earth began, as well as vegetable life, our atmosphere, the waters, the years, months and seasons, animal life, human life, sin, death...as well as the different races, nations and languages of people.

Although some have tried to find alternatives to the Biblical account of creation, they have failed to produce a single piece of scientific evidence to dispute the creation account ... or any other truth revealed in the Bible for that matter. True science and the Bible do not contradict one another.

But, despite the advancements of human intellect and technology, there still remains an unseen spiritual world beyond human comprehension to which we must refer to an "inspired" book written by an omniscient God for knowledge. The Bible reveals the existence of angels, evil spirits and a devil which scientific inquiry cannot refute or confirm beyond what the Bible reveals.

The Bible is a book that reveals itself as the written words of the one true God in which He reveals His will for our human family. It's origin, harmonious teachings, prophetical ability, and up-to-the-minute wisdom all support its credibility ...as do many other external confirmations.

The Bible, God's Revelation   *Chapter Three*

The Bible is the only written revelation of God's will for our human family...standing alone, above and beyond all other religious scriptures of man-made religions. Although multitudes of people rely upon other religious writings as their source of hope, the Bible is the only book that is proven to be the words of the one true God.

HOW WE GOT THE BIBLE

The first communication that God had with mankind was oral (word of mouth) communication, since writing had not yet been invented.

Beginning with Adam and Eve, God communicated His desires and orders by speaking directly to them. Adam and Eve heard the indisputable voice of God.

This oral communication was the way that God spoke to the first generations of our human family. Adam and Eve's two sons, Cain and Abel, were also familiar with God's voice, and later in history, God directly spoke to others as well ... people such as Noah, Abraham, Isaac and Jacob.

As history progressed God began to communicate to the masses of people through human prophets, who God personally chose as His spokesmen...to speak only those words He placed upon their lips. These prophets told others what God had told them, so that all people would know His message.

The Bible, God's Revelation   *Chapter Three*

In the book of Romans 1:1 we learn that "men of olden times were without excuse in knowing God and His will, since God has spoken to them both by His own lips and by the lips of His prophets, as well as by the things He has created" (my paraphrase).

Eventually writing was invented ... which God took advantage in sharing His message to the human family. An early example was when God directed Moses (one of the first Biblical writers) to record God's commandments for the children of Israel on tablets of stone.

Other men later followed Moses to speak and write the words of God as "they were moved by the Holy Spirit". In spite of their human weaknesses, the men chosen of God to record His words wrote an infallible record of what God told them.

Finally, after centuries of communicating through the Old Testament prophets, the time came for God's Son (Jesus) to visit the earth. His life on earth made the full will of God known to all mankind.

Jesus collected a group of disciples who He personally instructed, and with who He left the responsibility that they go into all the world and teach what they had learned from Him.

After Jesus ascended back to heaven these first disciples did as they were commanded...carrying His word throughout the then known world. And because these men spoke and wrote by the inspiration of God, they made no mistakes.

48

The Bible, God's Revelation   **Chapter Three**

God spoke to these early disciples directly through the Holy Spirit, who guided them to write the exact words God wanted them to write. It was God who gave them the wisdom that they recorded, making certain of no errors.

But while the original words of the Bible were Divinely inspired, this is not the promise regarding the various translations that would come later. Translators, at their very best, could not produce a perfect work. Yet, even though there are some minor errors in modern translations... the basic truths of God's word are still intact. Fortunately we have the Greek and Hebrew manuscripts to rely upon when in doubt.

A term often used in connection with the origin of the Bible is "canon". The word means "standard" or "rule". The sacred canon includes only those books that have passed the rigorous test, or standard, for Divinely inspired writings. These are the 66 books included in the Bible, each of which has passed the test of canonicity many centuries ago.

There were five rigorous outlines that each writing had to pass in order that they be acknowledged as inspired from God. These tests were all applied to any writing identified as God's word given to His chosen prophet. Not only has God taken great care in seeing that His truths were properly recorded, He also has taken precise care that those truths were properly preserved for all future generations. God has promised, "Heaven and earth shall pass away; but my words shall not pass away".

49

The Bible, God's Revelation   *Chapter Three*

It is truly miraculous that any part of the Bible remains for us to read when we remind ourselves of the subtle and severe attacks against it, and against God's church throughout the centuries. The bloody persecutions of the Christians were never as great as those times during the reign of the Roman Emperor, Diocletian, who in 303 A.D commanded that all the sacred books of the Christians be searched out and burned.

But even though the order was carried out, God saw to it that copies were made and preserved before many of the valuable manuscripts were destroyed.

It was Carlyle who said, "No lie can live forever". The fact that the Bible is still with us is strong evidence of its veracity, even though many attempts have been made to destroy and discredit it.

"Forever, O Lord, thy word is settled in heaven".

Psalms 119:89 (KJV)

In the times of Jesus every Jewish community had the part of the Bible we know as the Old Testament. It was handwritten on scrolls and kept in the synagogue where people met for religious instruction and worship. The scrolls were made from goatskins or sheepskins, sewn together to make rolls from ten to thirty feet long. During His earthly ministry Jesus read from one of these scrolls in the synagogue at Nazareth.

The Bible, God's Revelation   *Chapter Three*

Originally, the Old Testament books were written in the Hebrew language but, by the time of Christ, these Old Testament books had been translated into Greek, which was an international language at that time.

The first four books of the New Testament are known as the "gospels", which means "good news". They are so called because they tell of Jesus, the Christ, who came to earth sharing God's good news of salvation.

The New Testament also tells the experiences of Jesus' early followers as they went into the world to minister the good news of Christ as they were commanded.

The New Testament also contains letters written by the apostle Paul, and other apostles, to the early Christian churches throughout the Mediterranean world. Copies of these letters were made for neighboring churches also to read...providing Christian instruction for the new converts. These letters, along with copies of the gospel writings, were widely circulated throughout the Roman Empire, even though the early Christians were exposed to persecution.

When the United States became a nation in 1776, Bibles still had to be imported from England and Holland and were difficult to obtain. A Philadelphia printer named Robert Aitken produced the first English Bible ever printed in America. It was an edition of the King James Version that was commended to the public by a special Congressional resolution.

51

The Bible, God's Revelation   *Chapter Three*

Our country's forefathers valued the Holy Scriptures so highly that in 1816 they founded the American Bible Society to translate and publish the Bible, and to encourage its circulation. Its first president was Elias Boudinot, a friend of George Washington and president of the Continental Congress.

In later history, as scholarship considerably advanced, new versions helped to improve upon earlier versions. More original manuscripts have been discovered and the older ones are better understood. Archeological discoveries have also helped to illuminate certain portions of scripture.

HOW WE KNOW
THE BIBLE IS TRUE

Before we look at some of the answers to the question of the Bible's validity, let me confess that the evidence is so substantial and endless that our treatment of it here is but a mere overview. Even as we speak, new scientific discoveries continue to support and confirm the truths of this timeless book. We can place the evidence into two categories...internal evidence and external evidence.

INTERNAL EVIDENCE
THE CLAIMS OF THE BIBLE WRITERS AND JESUS

The Bible, God's Revelation   *Chapter Three*

The first internal evidence is that the Bible makes the claim that it is the word of God. This claim should not be taken lightly, especially when we consider the consequences. On several thousand occasions, the writers of the Bible reveal their words to be direct from God.

> "All scripture is given by inspiration of God, and *is* profitable for doctrine, for reproof, for correction, for instruction in righteousness: That the man of God may be perfect, thoroughly furnished unto all good works.."
>
> 2 Timothy 3:16-17 (KJV)

The Greek word for "inspiration" means "breathed into", or "out of". In other words, it means that God breathed out His words into the minds of the writers, so that they recorded only those things that God had spoken to them. Another passage that clarifies this Divine inspiration

> "For the prophecy came not in old time by the will of man: but holy men of God spake as they were moved by the Holy Ghost.."   2 Peter 1:21 (KJV)

Another claim that the Bible is Divinely inspired is from Jesus himself, who declared on various occasions that the scriptures were God given. Refer to: Mark 7:13, Matthew 5:18, John 10:35, John 14:26, John 6:12-14.

53

The Bible, God's Revelation   *Chapter Three*

QUESTION: Could all of the Bible writers over a period of 1600 years, who had no idea what the other writers had written, have recorded the identical lie to perpetrate a deceptive hoax? Or must their claims be true, that God did inspire them to record His words in a harmonious message?

And what about Jesus? If He is indeed the true Son of God as the Bible claims Him to be, then He becomes the supreme authority of the credibility of the scriptures. His word alone substantiates the validity of the Bible, for Jesus has emphatically stated the Bible to be God's word.

THE UNITY OF THE BIBLE'S MESSAGE

Another internal evidence to the Bible's credibility is its harmony of message. Forty different writers over a long period of history (16 centuries) have all written the same message, using the same characters, and revealing the same outcome. There are no contradictions or confusions about what they have written. Every writer agrees in perfect harmony with the whole message of the book. This alone suggests that a Divine Mind must have constructed it all.

THE SUPERIOR QUALITY
OF BIBLICAL TEACHING

54

The Bible, God's Revelation   *Chapter Three*

Not only are the teachings of the Bible in perfect harmony; they are also of superior quality. No other book that has ever been written...religious or otherwise...compares to the wisdom of the Bible.

While some people try to compare the teachings of the Bible with those of Zoroaster, Buddha, Confucius, Socrates, Mohammed, and a number of other religious and philosophical authors... the differences between other writings and the Bible are most profound. The Bible has in it nothing but truth ... while other religious writings are mixed with truth and error.

The Bible contains all truth ... so that no other truth is required on moral and spiritual topics that are not found in God's word. Science and history are lesser topics of importance for human meaning and purpose. When we refer to "all truth", we refer to the truth that has "profound and eternal" meaning. This cannot be said of any other writing, religious or otherwise.

Even if all the literature of ancient and modern times was gathered together...and all the beautiful thoughts of human philosophers and religionists were incorporated into one book ... they would not compare with the wisdom of God's word.

The wisdom of the Bible is beyond human ability to compose. It contains the most profound revelations of human life, of human need and human pain recorded anywhere ... yet it reveals these profound wisdoms in a language that is simple for us to understand.

The power of Biblical teaching, when understood and followed, has the ability to transform a human life. It has the power to meet every basic human need and desire for which mankind searches ... such as the need for true happiness, perfect peace, security, stability, fulfillment, and eternal hope.

EXTERNAL EVIDENCE

The internal evidence of the Bible is overwhelming. Its claims, its unity of message, and the timeless wisdom of its teachings are powerful witnesses to its truth and credibility. But internal evidence is not the only witness that we have. There are also external evidences that support the Bible as God's word.

Some of these external evidences are briefly touched on here as a review of how modern life and continuing education corroborate the credibility of God's word.

As scientific knowledge continues to advance, so does the reality that the Bible is correct and accurate in every thing it teaches. Few people outside the scientific community realize how dependent science has become on the Bible for our scientific achievements. Although the Bible was not written as a book of science, the wisdom and historical facts within it are great assets to scientific research.

Archaeology, for example, owes its success of ancient civilization discoveries to the Bible...which has been the road

The Bible, God's Revelation   *Chapter Three*

map to past cultures. Many recent discoveries from the ruins of Biblical cities confirm the Biblical narratives. Even those things that seemed most like a myth are being proven to have been factual, such as the great flood in Noah's day, which has now been irrefutably proven to be a scientific fact.

Narratives recorded in the Bible, which once were questionable because of lack of proof, are now being proven through scientific research as totally reliable. The more that science learns, the more the Bible is substantiated as trustworthy.

We could not list in this one study the many evidences that medicine, nutrition, psychiatry, farming, economics and all other disciplines of our modern time have contributed to the support of the Bible as a book without error.

We're talking about a miraculous book that could not have been put together by a group of mere human beings.

FULFILLED PROPHECIES

One of the amazing powers of the Bible is its ability to see into the future, to record in perfect detail events that would take place centuries after they were prophesied.

In the Old Testament, which was written many centuries before the birth and life of Jesus, there are some 300 prophecies that reveal every aspect of His life long before He was born.

57

The Bible, God's Revelation   *Chapter Three*

There are prophecies that revealed how Jesus would be born, where He would be born, the exact date He would be born, the killing of the infants by the evil king who sought to kill the infant Jesus, His life of ministry in detail, His betrayal by a friend who sold him for thirty pieces of silver, His cruel trial, His crucifixion on a cross before such a death was invented, His resurrection and His ascension back to heaven.

All these things and more were prophesied many centuries before Jesus was born. Jesus fulfilled every single prophecy in minute detail.

Other Old Testament prophecies provide exact detail for the outcome of different ancient cities and nations, i.e. Tyre, Sidon, Samaria, Moab, Ammon, Gaza, Ashkelon, Petra, Edom, Ninevah, Babylon, Thebes, Memphis, Chorazin, Bethsaida, Capernaum, Jerusalem, Palestine.

Historical documentation of the outcome of these cities and nations has proven these prophecies to be totally accurate.

Jesus also, while living on earth, prophesied of things that would occur in the future. He foretold the destruction of Jerusalem ... an event that happened 37 years after His death and resurrection.

Jesus also told of a time when the Jews would recapture Jerusalem after 2500 years of Gentile control. That prophesy was fulfilled in 1967 by the great six day war ... precisely in detail as Jesus prophesied 2000 years ago.

58

The Bible, God's Revelation   *Chapter Three*

The book of Revelation also foretells important events that have taken place long after the Revelation was written... including political and religious events from the year 33 A.D. until the second coming of Christ. Most of those prophecies have been fulfilled in the 2000 years since Jesus.

History has fully confirmed the amazing ability of the Revelation to see into the future.

PROPHETICAL CREDIBILITY

QUESTION: "Could the Bible prophecies have been written after the event...i.e. the prophecies relating to the Messiah written after the life and death of Jesus?"

ANSWER: The historic date for the completion of the Old Testament is accepted to be 450 years <u>before</u> the birth of Jesus. The Septuagint, which is the Greek translation of the Hebrew Old Testament, was completed in the reign of Ptolemy Philadelphus (285-246 B.C.). A Greek translation would not be possible without a prior Hebrew version. Any event described in the Old Testament that occurred after the date of 450 B.C. must be accepted as a fulfillment of Old Testament prophecy.

The New Testament was written prior to the second century A.D. Any event beyond that date must be considered as a fulfillment of New Testament prophecy.

59

The Bible, God's Revelation   *Chapter Three*

MATHEMATICAL PROBABILITIES

The probability of just one of those prophecies being fulfilled is 1 in 5,000,000,000. The mathematical probability that all the prophecies of the Bible would be fulfilled as given is beyond calculation. Yet, not just one, but every Biblical prophecy has been precisely fulfilled as it was given.

We could question the credibility of Biblical prophecy if just one of the events did not occur as prophesied, but that is not the situation.

Who, but God, could provide such miraculous prophetical ability?

The precise ability to see future events is beyond human ability, and must be regarded as coming from a Divine Being who has wisdom far exceeding that which human beings possess.

CONCLUSION

Does the Bible provide credible evidence to the existence of God? Those who take a "scientific" approach to research believe it more than satisfies the criteria of acceptability.

CONSIDER THIS...

The Bible, God's Revelation   *Chapter Three*

1.   No group of writers, living in different generations, could have put together such a precise and accurate record of events without corroboration...unless God inspired them to do so.

2.   No human intelligence is capable of developing such an exaggerated story line with such sublime characters as recorded in the Bible...unless God inspired them to do so.

3.   Evil dictators and new age scholars recognize the Bible to be more than a myth and have repeatedly tried to destroy the Bible's message and credibility...while never attempting to challenge any other writing. Wonder why they choose only to challenge the Bible...unless they realize this amazing book is, indeed, the writings of those inspired of God.

4.   History does not lie and has confirmed the remarkable ability of the Bible's author to prophesy events before they occur. Only God could see into the future with perfect accuracy, which He recorded by using His human writers as He inspired them to do so.

5.   The perennial wisdom and relevance of the Bible is beyond human intellect, yet mere humans have recorded insights so powerful that their lessons have endured as timeless throughout the ages...as God inspired them to do so.

61

The Bible, God's Revelation   **Chapter Three**

6.   There are no errors or contradictions of message, historical content, persons or events in the Bible... because God is the Author who inspired His writers to record only that which He knows to be true.

Why do I believe and trust in the existence of God? He has personally taken the time to write a book that reveals Himself and His will to the human family. He made certain that we not be confused about life.

Everywhere we look, reality just keeps getting better and better.

Jesus, The Christ, God's Revelation　　　　　*Chapter Four*

God's Third Revelation
Of Himself
To Our Human Family...

Jesus, The Christ
(Messiah)

A miraculous event has taken place. A man was born 2000 years ago. His name was Jesus...and He was either who he claimed to be (God on earth) ... or he was the perpetrator of the greatest hoax that mankind has ever witnessed.

For those who wish to know the truth, there is a way to distinguish between the two possibilities. In another writing we explore the numerous confirmations...beyond what the Bible teaches...that declare Jesus to be who He claimed to be. In this writing we introduce the person and evidence in His support.

CONSIDER THIS...

Jesus, The Christ, God's Revelation   **Chapter Four**

ONE SOLITARY LIFE

(Author unknown)

"He was born in an obscure village, the child of a peasant woman. He grew up in another obscure village, where He worked in a carpenter shop until He was thirty. Then for three years He was an itinerant preacher. He never had a family or owned a home. He never set foot inside a big city. He never traveled two hundred miles from the place He was born. He never wrote a book, or held an office. He did none of the things that usually accompany greatness.

While He was still a young man, the tide of popular opinion turned against Him. His friends deserted Him. He was turned over to His enemies, and went through the mockery of a trial. He was nailed to a cross between two thieves. While He was dying, His executioners gambled for the only piece of property He had --- His coat. When He was dead, He was taken down and laid in a borrowed grave.

Nineteen centuries have come and gone, and today He is the central figure for much of the human race. All the armies that ever marched, and all the navies that ever sailed, and all the parliaments that ever sat, and all the kings that ever reigned, put together, have not affected the life of man upon this earth as powerfully as this "One Solitary Life".

Jesus, The Christ, God's Revelation   **Chapter Four**

Ancient historians (Greek, Roman, Jewish) confirm the Biblical account of the life of Jesus. There is no dispute that Jesus lived and died the way the Bible reveals it to us. The only debate has been "Who was this Jesus of Nazareth?" On that question there are varied opinions.

Some ancients recognized Jesus as a great prophet and teacher of God similar in stature to the prophets of Old Testament times. Others of the established religious community believed that Jesus was a religious deceiver who sought to replace Judaism with his own religion. Others saw him as a rebellious zealot seeking to overthrow the Roman government.

These are some of the opinions that suggest Jesus was a fraud, and whose hoax was advanced through a group of followers who kept the deception going after his death. But for millions of people, from the earliest times of His public ministry, up to our present day, Jesus has been accepted to be who he claimed he was…the *only* and *unique* Son of God.

The Bible is very clear in its declaration of Jesus. It declares Him to be the only begotten Son of God who came to earth as the Messiah (Christ). In support of this Biblical declaration there are historical events that cannot be lightly dismissed.

The Bible uses some 260 names and titles to define the person of Jesus…all summarized in four of His titles…The Son of God, The Son of Man, The Messiah and The Prophet.

65

JESUS, THE SON OF GOD

There are 205 references in the Bible declaring Jesus to be The Son of God...emphasis on the word, "The". While all human beings may claim to be "sons and daughters of God", in that we are His physical creation...the Bible reveals only "One begotten of the Father" as The Spiritual Son who possessed the complete nature, attributes, power and authority of God. This One is identified to be Jesus of Nazareth.

JESUS, THE SON OF MAN

In contrast to being the Son of God, the Bible also reveals Jesus to be the Son of Man...which may sound confusing. Jesus was the physical son of Mary (but not Joseph) ...born through the birth process as other human beings. God had become man.

The birth of Jesus, as described in the Bible, was a miraculous event in which God's Holy Spirit impregnated a virgin woman.

Joseph, who was Mary's fiancée awaiting their marriage, was informed by a heavenly Angel that Mary had been selected to be the physical birth mother of God's Son...and that her pregnancy was not of human conception.

Jesus, The Christ, God's Revelation   **Chapter Four**

The question in some minds is..."Why didn't Jesus appear on earth in a miraculous revelation (like suddenly floating down from heaven in a cloud) to erase all doubt as to who He is?" The Bible answers that question in several places.

First of all, had Jesus chosen to enter the world through some mystical event, there would still be those who challenged and questioned that it actually happened. This is human nature... to be skeptical of mystical religious events...especially when the people of that day had already settled on their own religions and "gods".

Another reason for His natural birth was that it would be a more compelling evidence of Jesus' credibility when he fulfilled all the prophecies spoken centuries before...prophecies that began with the sign of the virgin birth spoken some seven hundred years prior to Jesus' birth.

One of the reasons that God chose a physical virgin birth was...so that it would be a clear sign to identify His Son beyond doubt. But that alone was not sufficient evidence...as such a birth could have been a mythical proclamation of his followers...much like the fantasy tales of other religious leaders.

There have been many self-proclaimed "saviors of mankind" throughout history, but all are proven to be counterfeit...ordinary men of ordinary parents. The virgin birth of Jesus was different. It confirmed Jesus as someone special.

67

Jesus, The Christ, God's Revelation   **Chapter Four**

The virgin birth is one of many prophecies regarding the coming Messiah (Christ) that was fulfilled in the life of Jesus. Those prophecies were recorded hundreds of years before the birth of Christ. Their fulfillment is a potent confirmation to the credibility of Jesus.

But there was another reason for the physical birth of Jesus. God wanted to experience what human beings experience. God, a spiritual Being, is far removed from the circumstances of human struggles. He wanted to understand the fullness of what humans experience...including birth, life and death.

God became human to understand human dilemma... especially our dilemma with sin. In order to do that God chose to experience every phase of human life, beginning at birth and continuing through adulthood.

JESUS, THE MESSIAH

The words "Messiah" and "Christ" mean the same thing and refer to the same person (The Anointed One). "Messiah" is the Hebrew term while "Christ" is the Greek translation.

The Old Testament contains prophecies of a Messiah who would eventually come to earth as the negotiator between God and man. The New Testament identifies Jesus of Nazareth to be that Messiah who fulfilled all the Old Testament prophecies.

68

Jesus, The Christ, God's Revelation   **Chapter Four**

While the Jewish community still looks for their Messiah to come as a "political" savior for their nation against their political enemies...Jesus has come as a "spiritual" savior to all mankind. This is the reason Jesus was rejected by the Jewish leadership. They looked for a political Messiah rather than a spiritual one. Jesus did not overthrow the Roman government as the Jews had expected of their Messiah.

JESUS, THE PROPHET

The words "prophet" and "prophesy" are used in two distinct ways in the scriptures. One refers to an "inspired speaker" (who speaks by Divine inspiration) and the other refers to "a fore teller" (who foretells or predicts future events).

The two-fold role of God's prophet is seen in scripture to "speak or teach by Divine inspiration" and to "foretell future events" as God revealed them. On occasion the prophet may speak inspired words (powerful truths) that do not include the foretelling of the future.

There have been men throughout history who were chosen of God as prophets...who spoke powerful truths as God inspired them to do. Some were also inspired to reveal future events long before they happened...events that were fulfilled hundreds and thousands of years after the life of the prophet.

69

Jesus, The Christ, God's Revelation   **Chapter Four**

But greater than any of these human prophets was "The Prophet" who would declare God's truths as never before spoken. This Prophet was Jesus, God's Son.

The two-fold role of a prophet was extraordinarily demonstrated in the life of Jesus. His message and revelations identify Jesus to be the most inspired teacher in all of human history. The truths that He taught are timely and eternal, to serve as the answer for all our human needs.

Jesus was also the most enlightened "seer of the future" that the world has ever known. He foretold future events so accurately that even the most critical skeptic must give respect to His prophetical ability. We look at His prophecies in great detail in the book entitled, "A Realistic Look At Jesus".

Understanding Jesus as "The Son of God", "The Son of Man", "The Messiah" and "The Prophet" is a beginning toward realizing who He is...and how He relates to our human family.

THE EXISTENCE OF JESUS
PRIOR TO HIS EARTHLY VISIT

There are forty-eight Bible references revealing the existence of Jesus prior to the creation of the universe. These references remind us that Jesus <u>did not</u> come into being at a baby's birth 2000 years ago in Bethlehem. Jesus has always been with his Father God before the creation of the universe.

70

Jesus, The Christ, God's Revelation   **Chapter Four**

THE EXISTENCE OF JESUS
DURING HIS EARTHLY VISIT

This is the part of Jesus' existence most familiar to us, since it is the part taught at length in the scriptures.

Hundreds of years prior to the birth of Jesus, the Old Testament prophets were given glimpses of His earthly visit. These prophecies deal with every aspect of His life...from His birth, to His death and resurrection. They are so explicit in detail that there can be no question that the historical Jesus of Nazareth is the One of who these prophecies refer.

The historical evidence of these fulfilled prophecies provides a powerful support to the credibility of the Bible's claim...that Jesus was indeed the Son of God who came to earth as our Messiah.

But, while the Bible provides details regarding the birth of Jesus, there is little known of His growing years other than one event when He was age twelve. Most of the revelations of Jesus' life on earth deal with his adult ministry and teaching.

The three-year earthly ministry of Jesus included His teaching and His healing miracles. But, as one of his disciples reveals...the earthly ministry of Jesus was so extensive that a complete library of books would not have told it all. (Refer to John 21:25)

71

Jesus, The Christ, God's Revelation   ***Chapter Four***

The four gospels provide a detailed record of thirty-five miracles that Jesus performed. Some tell of miraculous events with nature...such as the draught of fishes, stilling the storm, and walking on the water. Others tell of miraculous healings that include the healing of the blind, of the deaf and dumb, and of those with leprosy. Also recorded are the casting out of demons and the raising of the dead. On several occasions it is reported that multitudes of people brought their sick and afflicted to Jesus, who "healed every manner of disease and sickness"...although a detail of each one of these miracles was not recorded.

The miracles of Jesus were witnessed by huge gatherings of people that continued to grow in number as the word was spread of all that Jesus was capable of doing. Many realized that Jesus was more than just a human being, accepting that He was God, capable of all things. Others regarded His abilities only as a gift from God to fulfill His role as prophet.

Then there are the prophecies spoken by Jesus himself, which foretell future events...all of which have been historically fulfilled precisely as He spoke them.

The prophetical ability of Jesus, linked to His ability to perform miracles beyond human understanding, is a strong evidence of Jesus' authority as a Divine Being in human form.

But there still is another evidence of His divinity that cannot be dismissed... the message of Jesus.

Jesus, The Christ, God's Revelation   **Chapter Four**

The teachings of Jesus are so profound and timely that they could literally change our entire world if they were honored and followed. The truths that Jesus unveiled have never been duplicated in all of human wisdom. He understood God with an intimacy that no other person has ever revealed...and He understands mankind far more than we understand ourselves.

Jesus knew the needs of our human family, as well as our problems...and He knew the solutions. Those who follow His teachings enjoy a full and meaningful existence...even in the complex and evil world in which we live.

The two most in-depth recorded lessons of Jesus are His "sermon on the mount", recorded in Matthew, chapters 5,6,7 and His "final address to His followers", recorded in John, chapters 14,15,16.

The wisdom and revelations of these two sermons are so remarkably pure and pertinent to human life, that literary and historical scholars regard them as the "greatest published literature" in all of the known writings throughout history.

There has never been a teacher with such profound wisdom as that expressed by this "simple" man born in an obscure village some 2000 years ago. Even today, His teachings are the most revered and followed of all teachings combined.

But there still remained a most profound thing that Jesus did...which became the most significant event in all of human history...and is the ultimate confirmation of His deity...

73

Jesus, The Christ, God's Revelation   **Chapter Four**

THE DEATH OF JESUS

The days of sorrow came when the historical Jesus was captured, tried and crucified by the religious and political leaders. The question is, why? If Jesus is God's son, why did God allow him to be punished and persecuted as He was?

What is so remarkable about the life of Jesus, including His death, is that it was all prophesied centuries before he was born. The amazing prophecy of Jesus' death (described by Isaiah 700 b. c.) revealed <u>how</u> Jesus would be crucified...even though punishment by crucifixion was <u>not yet invented</u> in Isaiah' time.

God not only revealed that the Messiah would be crucified at a certain future date...He also described the manner of crucifixion which had not yet been conceived by evil men.

According to the Bible, the purpose for the cruel death of Jesus was as a sacrifice for the sins of mankind. Although at the hands of men, it was in the plan and permission of God that His only Son be offered up as a sacrifice.

The Bible teaches us, that God demands the shedding of blood for the remission of sin. This was accomplished in the Old Testament era through animal sacrifices...offered up once every year. But the yearly animal sacrifices were only representations of the true sacrifice, God's Son, who would shed His blood once and for all ...that the sins of all mankind could be forgiven... made available for those who desired forgiveness.

74

Jesus, The Christ, God's Revelation Chapter Four

THE RESURRECTION

OF JESUS

Jesus did not remain dead for very long, however. The Bible declares that Jesus resurrected from the dead after three days in the grave. The question is, did it really happen or did His disciples just concoct the story? Let's review the evidence.

1.   The political and religious authorities of Jesus' day had a serious problem on their hands when Jesus returned to life three days after He was crucified. The masses of people were now convinced that Jesus was telling the truth and that their Messiah had been wrongly judged and crucified by their religious and political leaders.

To cover up their crime, the politicians and priests conspired to make up a false story that the body of Jesus had been stolen from the grave by His disciples after the Roman soldier guards had conveniently fallen asleep. Their story had many loopholes and was never accepted by the people.

2.   Had the Roman guards, who were assigned to guard the tomb of Jesus, fallen asleep at their post as the fake story suggested...their superiors would have put them to death as punishment. This was an unalterable law of the Roman army ...no one slept at their post. But no guard was ever punished.

75

Jesus, The Christ, God's Revelation   **Chapter Four**

3.   Had the guards actually fallen asleep, how could a few men have rolled away the huge stone that covered the grave entrance without the use of oxen...doing it so quietly as not to disturb one single guard lying asleep next to the grave?

4.   Had the disciples been successful in doing this, why was there never an all out search by the Roman and Jewish officials to make certain to recover the body of Jesus? Why was not one disciple brought before the court to confess what they did with the body? Instead of being questioned by the leaders once the body was discovered as missing, the disciples were left alone as they preached in public places to the masses of people...telling them that Jesus had resurrected...while the religious and political leaders looked helplessly on in amazement and fear.

5.   Had the disciples stolen and hidden the body of Jesus, why was there never anyone in their group to betray their hoax by revealing it to the authorities? Surely, one person would not have given their life for a fantasy they knew to be false.

6.   Where is the body of Jesus? Had the disciples stolen the body of Jesus...where in the world would they have hidden it so that it would never be recovered? Would it not still be the top priority of every religion on earth to uncover the body of Jesus to prove that He was a hoax...if they really believed He was?

Jesus, The Christ, God's Revelation   **Chapter Four**

The reality is, no one has ever looked...even from the moment of the disciples' cries ... "He has risen from the dead".

7.   Had the disciples stolen and hidden the body of Jesus... to cover up a hoax that was started by a now dead man...why would they eventually suffer imprisonment, beatings and death for a lie? No one would die if they really had known that Jesus was a deceiver and hoax.

Every disciple of Jesus could have been spared their sufferings and death by simply ceasing to preach that Jesus had resurrected from the dead. They could have lived to ripe old ages by simply turning over the body of Jesus to the officials. But no one did.

The disciples died for their teaching because they knew the truth ...Jesus was alive. They had seen Him, conversed with Him, and were being empowered by His Spirit to preach those things they knew for certain were true. Physical punishment and death was a small price to pay to share the message of a living Savior.

CONCLUSION...

The evidence is overwhelming...Jesus of Nazareth did, indeed, resurrect from the dead three days after His crucifixion ...just as the prophets, and Jesus Himself, proclaimed He would do. This fact alone is proof of His Divinity...that Jesus was exactly who He claimed to be...God in the flesh.

Jesus, The Christ, God's Revelation   **Chapter Four**

THE EXISTENCE OF JESUS
NOW...IN OUR PRESENT TIME

Two thousand years ago a man named Jesus walked on the earth...healing all manner of disease and teaching powerful truths of hope for our human family. The religious and political leaders killed him...not because of His rebellion against the state...but because of His message of love. Three days after His crucifixion, Jesus resurrected from the dead. Where is He now?

According to the Bible, Jesus returned to heaven where he now sits at the right hand of God, making intercession to God for all mankind. He is the Lord of the universe and Head of the true Church that He created...which is alive and well...and which is under the watchful eye of Jesus.

The man, Jesus, was more than just a man. He was God, who came to earth to reveal our Creator's love and compassion.

SUMMARY

Does the life of Jesus provide credible evidence to the existence of God? Those who take a "scientific" approach to research believe it more than satisfies the criteria of acceptability. Here is the summary of facts...

Jesus, The Christ, God's Revelation   **Chapter Four**

1.   Historical accounts, beyond the Bible's record, confirm the authenticity of Jesus' life. For sure, He lived and ministered 2000 years ago, just as the Bible reveals it.

2.   Jesus is either who He claimed to be or else He has perpetrated the greatest hoax in all of human history.

But the evidence is overwhelming in support of His declaration, and nothing has been offered in the last two thousand years to suggest otherwise. Archaeological and historical discoveries ... as well as modern events now taking place... continue to mount evidence in support of the Bible's accuracy and Jesus' credibility.

3.   Even a skeptical religious leader had to admit to Jesus, "We know that you are a great teacher from God...for no man can do these miracles except God be with Him." Even this skeptic in Jesus' day knew there was something different about Jesus and his teachings.

This would also have to be the conclusion of anyone who accepts the miracles of Jesus described in the Bible...for no ordinary human being possesses the ability to do what Jesus has done. The Biblical record of what He did stands as evidence to His Divine nature.

Jesus, The Christ, God's Revelation   ***Chapter Four***

4.   Yet, beyond His miracles, the life and teachings of Jesus are equally powerful testaments to His credibility. The way He lived and the message He taught are far superior to any other historical religious teacher...or any other human for that matter.

The history of other religious leaders reveals the reality that they had personal ambitions that transcended the needs and welfare of others. Some even chose militant means to advance their objectives...but this was never the teaching or activity of Jesus. His life and message are the essence of love and compassion. He gave His life to save yours.

5.   The love of Jesus, His teaching of love, and His non-militant, non-political sacrifice identify Him to be someone of far superior motive than those of human activists. Jesus came to reveal God and to make a way by which we could be reconciled to God's fellowship...even when we have sinned and fallen short of God's will. No one has ever loved the human family that much. His motives, actions and message are pure and eternal evidence to His credibility.

6.   Jesus lived and ministered during the time of the oppressive government of the Roman Empire. Even the Jewish nation where He ministered was under Roman rule...that allowed the Jewish people their religious rituals as a political convenience. Whatever was done in Israel was done under the

80

Jesus, The Christ, God's Revelation   **Chapter Four**

watchful eye of the Roman officials, as well as the Jewish religious hierarchy who had befriended the Romans rulers.

The life and message of Jesus was antagonistic to the self-exalted position of the Jewish religious leaders. Had the Jewish leaders accepted Jesus as the Messiah, their position would have been in jeopardy, both with the Jews and with the Romans. For that reason the religious leaders did everything in their power to discredit and destroy the life and message of Christ. But even after they convinced the Romans to kill Jesus, the Jewish leadership had to deal with His resurrection and with His followers who continued to preach in His name.

Using their political influence with the Romans, the religious leaders harassed, imprisoned and put to death those who would not denounce Jesus. Every one of the original twelve disciples, except John, was murdered for their preaching about Jesus. John's fate was to be put in exile on the island of Patmos, where he lived alone to an advanced old age.

The Jews publicly stoned another disciple, Stephen, to death...because of his testimony for Christ. The apostle Paul, who had once been part of the Jewish leadership in trying to destroy the Christians, became a convert himself...and was eventually beheaded by the Romans because of his preaching that Jesus was the Christ.

Even at the expense of personal safety, all the early followers of Christ who witnessed His death, continued to teach

Jesus, The Christ, God's Revelation　　　　　　　**Chapter Four**

everywhere that Jesus was the Messiah who had risen from the dead...even though they were certain of personal suffering.

Why? Because they knew the truth ... Jesus was the God He claimed to be. They would never denounce the One who came to earth to free mankind from our enslavement to sin.

7.　　　Throughout the centuries, the followers of Christ have endured imprisonment, cruel and inhumane punishment, and even death at the hands of political powers and religionists...yet they all remained faithful to their allegiance to Christ.

Why? The answer is basic...they knew beyond a shadow of a doubt that Jesus was the promised Christ of God... and they were willing to give their lives so that His message would be advanced.

No man would die for a hoax. The fact that the early disciples, who were personal witnesses to the life and teachings of Jesus, would give their lives for His cause is a powerful testimony to the credibility of Jesus. The fact that countless numbers of true Christians throughout the centuries have suffered and died for the message of Christ is a powerful testimony to the credibility of Jesus. The fact that people today continue to be harassed...and are even put to death for their allegiance to Christ...is a powerful testimony to the credibility of Jesus. No man or woman would die for a hoax.

Jesus, The Christ, God's Revelation   ***Chapter Four***

8.   During His earthly ministry Jesus prophesied future events so precisely that they continue to amaze scholars even today. Their fulfillment is certain proof of His Godly status. The most famous of His prophecies is that of the destruction of Jerusalem, recorded in Matthew 24:1-22 and Luke 21:6-24.

Standing in front of the temple at Jerusalem, Jesus announced to His followers that the Roman gentiles would destroy the city and temple. His prophecy was delivered during a time of total peace. There were no uprisings or wars anywhere in the world at the time of His announcement. The Jews at that time were enjoying peace with the Romans without any threat to their land or religious freedom. Why then would Jesus make such a prophecy? From where did He get His information?

Jesus knew that the Roman army would destroy Jerusalem, because Jesus was God who knew all things. No man could have predicted the coming calamity with such clarity and accuracy. He even described the atrocious events that would take place at the hands of the invading soldiers...referring to it as "a great tribulation such as the world has never seen".

Thirty-seven years after His death, this prophecy came true in precise detail...just as Jesus had warned. Titus, the Roman general, led his army's attack upon Jerusalem with the force and animosity of animals.

Even today's warlords shake their heads at the merciless and brutal conduct of the Romans. Never in all the chronicles of

83

Jesus, The Christ, God's Revelation   Chapter Four

war has there been such cruelty displayed on a people as that by Titus upon the Jews at Jerusalem in 70 A.D. ...just as Jesus predicted 37 years earlier.

But there are also other prophecies of Jesus that continue to be fulfilled even in our current time. His wisdom in understanding future events is a strong proof that Jesus is who He claimed to be...the Son of God who knows all things.

SO, THEN...

Although there are many skeptics who would prefer to avoid the Divinity of Jesus, no one has yet provided any evidence in the last 2000 years to challenge the historical record of Jesus. The more we advance in scientific knowledge, the more we come to realize how absolute, real and accurate the Bible truly is...and how precisely perfect the Bible has revealed God and His Son, Jesus the Christ.

The life, teaching and resurrection of Jesus are powerful and miraculous revelations of God. As a researcher I cannot avoid the remarkable and abundant evidence of the life of Jesus as a confirmation to the existence of God.

Everything in God's perfect plan for mankind fits together in perfect harmony...precisely as the Bible reveals it.

Why do I believe in God? I believe...because He has revealed Himself in the purity and power of Jesus, the Christ.

Everywhere we look, reality just keeps getting better and better.

The Holy Spirit, God's Revelation　　　　　　*Chapter Five*

God's Fourth Revelation
Of Himself
To Our Human Family...

The Holy Spirit

A miraculous event is taking place. Someone is following you around as you go through life...talking with you where no one else can listen in. There is a voice within you that you have heard all of your life. It is the voice of God's Spirit.

You may not have recognized the voice, and even brushed it aside, thinking it to be your inner conscience...but God has been speaking to you for a long time. He has been telling you that there is more to life...and that there is Someone who is available to help you get the most from it.

That's the same voice we all have heard ...every human being who has ever been born...because every person is special to God.

God's Holy Spirit is a friend. He encourages us and He criticizes us. He congratulates us when we do things right and He convicts us when we do things wrong.

The Holy Spirit, God's Revelation   ***Chapter Five***

The Holy Spirit is speaking directly to you in the innermost secret domain of your life...where only you and He have access. His purpose is to guide you toward a deeper relationship with your Creator.

This fact alone reveals how special you are to God...that the Creator of the universe would actually take the time and the interest to privately visit with you in the person of the Holy Spirit...to help you enjoy the blessings He has in store for you... both for this life and the life to come.

> For as many as are led by the Spirit of God, they are the sons of God.   Romans 8:14 (KJV)

Throughout the Bible we are introduced to the Holy Spirit by the various ministries He performs in our behalf. Each of these ministries is for the sole purpose of helping us succeed at this thing we call "life". It is because of the Holy Spirit that the apostle Paul could proclaim, "We are more than conquerors through Him who loves us". One Of His ministries is that of ...

CONVICTOR

The Holy Spirit is extremely active in the salvation of all mankind. While we are still rebellious sinners against God, the Holy Spirit visits with us as bearer of three urgent messages...

The Holy Spirit, God's Revelation   *Chapter Five*

The first message of the Holy Spirit reveals our problem in our relationship with our Creator. In other words, the Holy Spirit convicts us that we are sinners...revealing to us that we disrespect the authority of our Creator to rebel against His laws.

This conviction creates an inner guilt that tells us something is wrong with our life. The guilt we feel is actually a blessing from God's Spirit...to remind us that there is Someone to who we must give ultimate account.

The second message of The Holy Spirit reveals the anger and ultimate justice of God. This is an area of God's character that some people have difficulty in understanding and which we will deal with at length later in this writing. The question often heard is, "How could a good God send someone to an eternal punishment in hell?"

The Holy Spirit's message is that there will be an ultimate judgment by a righteous God who is angry with those who rebel against His authority and Supremacy. Knowing that a judgment is imminent produces an inner fear that we cannot escape. It is God's mercy that warns us of His impending judgment, so that we may have the opportunity to seek His help beforehand.

The third message of the Holy Spirit is that there is a hope to the sinner who desires to be forgiven of our rebellion against our Creator. The Holy Spirit offers an assurance that God is merciful to offer His plan for our salvation...if we desire it.

The Holy Spirit, God's Revelation   **Chapter Five**

The "convicting" ministry of the Holy Spirit is God's revelation to each of us privately...that He does indeed exist and that He is deeply interested in our welfare.

God, in the person of the Holy Spirit, is very aggressive to lure us back to Himself by revealing to us that something is wrong with our life. That inner voice is a blessed gift from God, because He loves us enough to show us our error. Without the knowledge that we are sinners in the court of God, mankind has no motivation to seek God's forgiveness.

The guilt and fear of being estranged from God is a necessary ingredient to our eternal salvation. The conviction of the Holy Spirit is the beginning of a new life with God. We are greatly privileged that God would visit us through His Spirit to draw us to Himself.

> (Words of Jesus) " Nevertheless I tell you the truth; It is expedient for you that I go away: for if I go not away, the Comforter (Holy Spirit) will not come unto you; but if I depart, I will send him unto you. And when he is come, he will reprove the world of sin, and of righteousness, and of judgment: ... I have yet many things to say unto you, but ye cannot bear them now. Howbeit when he, the Spirit of truth, is come, he will guide you into all truth: for he shall not speak of himself; but whatsoever he shall hear, *that* shall he speak: and he will show you things to come. He shall glorify me: for he shall receive of mine, and shall show *it* unto you.."   John 16:7-14 (KJV)

88

The Holy Spirit, God's Revelation   *Chapter Five*

EMPOWEROR

Conviction is not the only involvement of God's Spirit in our salvation experience. He also is the "spiritual power" by which our lives are converted from evil to righteousness.

As sinful human beings we have no wisdom or power to change our life style that is being controlled by our inner evil character. According to the Bible...and confirmed by historical reality...mankind is morally and spiritually corrupt. Our actions are dictated by the power of evil.

There is no pill or therapy in existence that can correct the problem of sin's power to change the inner character of the human heart. Only God can meet the need. In other words, we need a "spiritual" power to replace the evil power that currently controls our life. That spiritual power comes from the presence of God's Spirit, who takes residence in our life at our "conversion".

When a person responds to the Holy Spirit's conviction, to bow before God as a contrite sinner seeking forgiveness...not only does God forgive, He also changes (converts) the person.

This change is a spiritual miracle identified in the Bible as being "born again". This new birth (spiritual transformation) comes only from the power of the Holy Spirit's presence in our life.

The Holy Spirit, God's Revelation   **Chapter Five**

Prior to "conversion" the Holy Spirit visits with us from time to time to convict us. At conversion, the Holy Spirit takes up residence in our life as a permanent and powerful friend.

> Jesus answered and said unto him, Verily, verily, I say unto thee, Except a man be born again, he cannot see the kingdom of God. Nicodemus saith unto him, How can a man be born when he is old? can he enter the second time into his mother's womb, and be born? Jesus answered, Verily, verily, I say unto thee, Except a man be born of water and of the Spirit, he cannot enter into the kingdom of God. That which is born of the flesh is flesh; and that which is born of the Spirit is spirit. Marvel not that I said unto thee, Ye must be born again. The wind bloweth where it listeth, and thou hearest the sound thereof, but canst not tell whence it cometh, and whither it goeth: so is every one that is born of the Spirit.   John 3:3-8 (KJV)

The Bible uses various terms to identify the spiritual change in a person's life that has been accomplished by the Holy Spirit.

We are taught that the Holy Spirit "quickens" (makes spiritually alive) and that He "quenches our spiritual thirst". The Bible further states that the Holy Spirit "circumcises the heart" and "frees us from sin and spiritual death".

The Holy Spirit, God's Revelation   *Chapter Five*

Each of these phrases reminds us that sinful man is dependent upon God's Spirit to free us from the power of sin and to make us "new creatures" in Christ.

"Therefore if any man be in Christ, he is a new creature: old things are passed away; behold, all things are become new."   2 Corinthians 5:17

It is the Holy Spirit who "produces the power of righteousness" so that we can live above sin. (Romans 8:4-5, Galatians 5:5)

It is the Holy Spirit who "bears witness" that we are now God's children. (Romans 8:16)

It is the Holy Spirit who "washes, sanctifies and justifies" us in the eyes of God. (I Corinthians 6:11, Hebrews 9:14)

It is the Holy Spirit who "changes us into the glory of Christ". (II Corinthians 3:18).

It is the Holy Spirit who "strengthens us to witness, to overcome and to serve God and our fellowman". (Romans 8:3)

It is the Holy Spirit who "frees us from the Old Testament laws and rituals". (II Corinthians 3:13-18)

It is the Holy Spirit who "adds us to God's one true church, the Body of Christ". (Ephesians 2:19-22)

91

The Holy Spirit, God's Revelation   **Chapter Five**

COMFORTER, COUNSELOR
AND
TEACHER OF TRUTH

Jesus revealed to his followers that, after He returned to heaven, another Heavenly companion would take His place as they went forward to minister in His name. That companion would be the Holy Spirit...who would lead them, teach them, and empower them.

The success of the early Christian church in spreading the gospel of Christ throughout the world was the result of men led by the Spirit of God. Throughout history the Holy Spirit has been a companion with God's "born again" children...providing inner strength and wisdom that cannot be found from any other source.

(words of Jesus) "If ye love me, keep my commandments. And I will pray the Father, and he shall give you another Comforter, that he may abide with you for ever; Even the Spirit of truth; whom the world cannot receive, because it seeth him not, neither knoweth him: but ye know him; for he dwelleth with you, and shall be in you. I will not leave you comfortless: I will come to you. Nevertheless I tell you the truth; It is expedient for you that I go away: for if I go not away, the Comforter will not come unto you; but if I depart, I will send him unto you.

John 14:15-18; John 16:7 (KJV)

The Holy Spirit, God's Revelation   *Chapter Five*

Wisdom to separate truth from the current day confusion is God's blessing...available through the companionship of God's Holy Spirit. Every human being can know life's most profound truths that deal with "who we are, where we came from, why we exist, and where we are headed when life is over."

MINISTER

Throughout history the Holy Spirit has empowered ordinary people with special gifts and wisdom to perform extraordinary ministries in the name of God. For example...

Joseph was given a gift to interpret dreams...Bezalel was given gifts and skills to construct the Tabernacle...Moses and seventy elders were given wisdom to teach people as God's prophets...Balaam was given the gift of prophecy to edify God's people by foretelling future blessings...Joshua was given wisdom to carry on as Israel's leader after Moses...Samson was given physical strength against God's enemies...David was given great power as King of Israel.

Even the Lord Jesus (in human flesh) was empowered by the Holy Spirit (who was given without measure unto Him). Jesus was God's Son, sent for a special mission...but the human flesh that Jesus inhabited was ordinary and powerless to perform the tasks Jesus was called to do. Only through God's spirit could the human Jesus perform the works that only God can perform.

The Holy Spirit, God's Revelation   **Chapter Five**

The Holy Spirit came upon Jesus at His baptism by John. Soon after, the Holy Spirit led Jesus into the wilderness to be tempted of satan...providing the human Jesus with the power to overcome temptation. In His earthly ministry Jesus performed miracles and healings by the power of the Holy Spirit. He cast out devils by the Holy Spirit and gave God's commandments to the people by the Holy Spirit. The life and ministry of Jesus was totally consumed by the Holy Spirit of God.

Before He returned to heaven, Jesus revealed to His disciples that they too would be empowered with a special baptism of the Holy Spirit...in order that they could carry out the awesome ministry of spreading His gospel to a pagan world. This baptism of the Spirit on the disciples of Christ came about on the day of Pentecost after Jesus' ascension back to heaven.

These ordinary men, called to be the disciples of Jesus, became extraordinary prophets that converted the pagan world to the one true Christ. They went forth speaking by the inspiration of the Holy Spirit. They comforted others by the Holy Spirit. They became great witnesses, with great power, through the abiding presence of God's Spirit.

They dreamed dreams, saw visions and prophesied through the power of the Holy Spirit. They directed the business affairs of the early church through the leadership of the Holy Spirit. They even brought down harsh wrath and punishment on evil men and women through the Holy Spirit.

The Holy Spirit, God's Revelation   **Chapter Five**

No minister has since been so empowered, or accomplished so much, as those early disciples who were given a special anointing of God's Spirit so that they could go into a pagan world to share a new religion. The odds were overwhelming against them, yet they succeeded because they were ordinary men empowered by extraordinary gifts from the Holy Spirit.

PROTECTOR

God's Holy Spirit is ever present in the life of every born again believer. His presence provides strength, comfort and protection from all evil. Jesus promised...

> (words of Jesus)" And I will pray the Father, and he shall give you another Comforter, that he may abide with you for ever; Even the Spirit of truth; whom the world cannot receive, because it seeth him not, neither knoweth him: but ye know him; for he dwelleth with you, and shall be in you.." John 14:16-17 (KJV)

Although God's people have endured hardships on earth, even to the point of death by martyrdom, none of God's children are consumed by the evils of the world. God's Spirit is with them to help them remain faithful and loyal to their God.

The Holy Spirit, God's Revelation   ***Chapter Five***

The Holy Spirit is present to "guide us into all truth" (John 16:13, Luke 1:15) The Holy Spirit is present to "mortify the deeds of our body" (Romans 8:13) The Holy Spirit is present to "help us to pray" (Romans 8:26-27, Ephesians 2:18, 6:18, John 4:24) The Holy Spirit is present to "encourage us" by glorifying Jesus, showing us our inheritance and revealing God's blessings. (John 16:14, Ephesians 1:17, Galatians 4:6, Romans 8:16, I Corinthians 2:9) The Holy Spirit is present to "fill us with love, joy, peace, faith, patience, meekness" (Galatians 5:22-25) The Holy Spirit is present to "empower us in the inner man" (Ephesians 3:16, II Timothy 1:7) The Holy Spirit is present to "seal us in the faith" ... to "stamp" us as God's "property" or child. (II Corinthians 1:22)

The Holy Spirit is very active in human lives today…both in the lives of the "unsaved" as well as the "saved". Without the presence of the Holy Spirit, mankind has no hope. We are totally dependent upon Him for our eternal salvation, our wisdom, our courage, and for life's direction in a world that appears to have no direction. It is a most wise person who listens and follows the inner voice of God's loving Holy Spirit.

God is revealing Himself each and every day to each and every human being through His Spirit…speaking privately to us in the inner sanctuary of our heart and mind. Only a God of pure love would care that much to help a rebellious and sinful race. Everywhere we look, reality just keeps getter better and better.

96

Human Experiences, God's Revelation   **Chapter Six**

God's Fifth Revelation
Of Himself
To Our Human Family...

Human Experiences

Do miracles happen? Does God answer prayer? Can anyone prove miracles? Yes ... to all three questions. But first, we have to determine what a true miracle is and separate those who claim to have had a miracle from those who really have. Credibility is our first concern.

There are four groups of people who relate to God...atheists, non-believers, religionists and children. The distinction between these four groups will clear up many confusing questions about "true religion"...and about "miraculous interventions of God".

An atheist, or agnostic, chooses not to believe in the existence of a Divine Being, therefore seeks no relationship with one. They neither help nor hinder our search for God or for Divine miracles.

Human Experiences, God's Revelation   ***Chapter Six***

The term "non-believer" is used in religious circles to describe someone who does believe in God's existence...but chooses to cast aside any relationship or trust in Him. They also neither help nor hinder our search for God or God's miracles.

A "religionist" is someone who believes in God's existence...professes a form of religion...yet has no true relationship with God. This person may be very active in religious liturgy and church service...yet their daily life style does not bear the fruits of true religion. Some "religious" people are revealed to be hypocritical and sinful while maintaining their stern allegiance to a "religion" or "religious principle". These people are very confusing to someone who wants to understand God. Often these people describe miracles that are mysterious and mythical, rather than pure interventions of God.

Before we look at the fourth group of people who relate to God, let's step back and consider how a "true" miracle should be defined. In doing so, let's first look at false miracles.

FALSE MIRACLES

Throughout history people have claimed to experience a miracle in their life. Some of these claims involve "visions" while others involve healing, deliverance, or wisdom for making decisions.

98

Human Experiences, God's Revelation   *Chapter Six*

It is not within our human ability to confirm or deny these claims, yet there are some miracle claims that cannot be accepted within Biblical standards. God made a pointed observation and statement when He said...

"An evil generation seeks for signs. There will be no sign given except the sign of Jonah". (referring to the resurrection of Jesus)   Luke 11:29

In this statement God was saying in effect, "I am not going to try and prove myself to the human race by performing a bunch of miracles at the whim of those who demand a sign from heaven."

This declaration eliminates a lot of so-called miracles. For instance, when someone thinks they see a religious image in a cloud or in a shadow...or some other representation of a heavenly being, they are wrong. That is not the way God reveals Himself. And when someone declares that a stone statue begins to weep or shed blood, they too are wrong. God does not reveal Himself in such mythical expressions.

These are only a couple examples of many such "visions" which have enticed the curiosity of spiritually ignorant people, but you get the idea of what we're getting at. Such "miraculous" visions tend to discredit "real" miracles.

99

Human Experiences, God's Revelation   **Chapter Six**

TRUE MIRACLES

A true miracle is defined as "an event that is unexplainable by the natural laws of science and nature...to suggest it can only occur by a supernatural process as an act of God." No other explanation can be given for the event. With this in mind we turn our attention to the reality of miracles as experienced by credible people throughout history.

This brings us to the fourth group of people who relate to God ... the "children of God". The Bible describes a specific group of people as "children of God"...so called because of a "spiritual re-birth" that has "miraculously changed their life", to re-unite them to a relationship with God, the Father. These spiritual children are also referred to as "born-again" believers.

This group of people is distinguished from all other human beings because of their miraculous, life-changing experience that instantly removes their old ways of evil living... replacing them with a new and righteous life style. These "children" have experienced a personal relationship with God.

The testimony of millions of these people throughout the last 2000 years cannot be lightly overlooked. This is the group of voices that we can rely upon as a credible confirmation of God's miraculous interventions in their life...that include testimonies involving salvation, healing, deliverance, provision, guidance and ministry to others.

Human Experiences, God's Revelation   *Chapter Six*

Space does not permit an exhaustive review of true miracles that have been experienced by modern-day "children of God", but I will review a couple just for example. These are not the most profound miracles of record...they are listed just to identify what happens to those of faith.

CONFIRMED TESTIMONIES
OF MIRACLES

An elderly lady fell and damaged her knee so terribly that the doctors felt she would never walk again. Her pain was insufferable. A group of people gathered around her bed and prayed for healing. Immediately the woman arose from her bed and began to walk without pain. She never had any more trouble with her knee for the remainder of her life.

A man lay on his deathbed without any strength to get out of bed or even to talk. There was no medical hope for him. His family waited quietly by his bed for the end. A group of believing friends stopped by and prayed for him while "anointing" him with oil. Immediately the man's eyes opened, his strength returned, he began to talk, got out of bed and lived a normal, healthy life for many years following.

A woman who was pronounced dead by the doctors in the hospital dramatically returned to life to enjoy more years.

101

Human Experiences, God's Revelation   **Chapter Six**

A single mother of three children, without a job or income, was down to a few crackers and cheese when she knelt before God with a sincere prayer to help her feed her children. She had not discussed her plight with anyone...but shortly after she prayed, the phone rang as her aunt felt "compelled" to call and offer to bring over some food. The next day, after many weeks of frustration in trying to get a job, the phone rang again from a company who asked if she could begin work that evening. Coincidence? To those who know how God intervenes in the lives of His children, there's no question...it was no coincidence.

An 18-month-old child was so blind that she ran into objects continually. Glasses were required just to maintain her safety. A believing parent took the child to a church where the believers prayed for the healing of her eyesight. Immediately her eyes were healed and she never wore glasses again.

A medical doctor/surgeon testified to a miraculous return to life of his very own son...who had been clinically dead for four hours.

A well-known minister in our community had continuous trials of physical suffering, including terminal cancer. He was operated on between 25 and 30 times and was given up to die by the doctors on four different occasions. He even made out his funeral arrangements on two of those occasions. His troubles began as a teenager when he was

102

Human Experiences, God's Revelation   **Chapter Six**

diagnosed with bone cancer so severely that a leg bone had decayed in half. Yet, all the time I knew him in adult life he never walked oddly or gave any indication of any existing damage. The reason? ...a praying mother. He tells the story of how the doctors wanted to remove his leg to save his life, but he would not give permission. His mother prayed ... the cancer went away...and he walked from that time on two legs.

Later in life cancer was found in his intestinal tract. The doctors gave him 3 to 6 months to live and sent him home to die. A Christian lady prayed for his healing and told him to "go home and forget the cancer, God has healed you". Immediately, his excruciating pain left him. One year later he returned to the Lexington clinic where the doctors confirmed the healing at the amazement of the entire surgical staff.

This minister, throughout his life, experienced six physical miracles from certain death...cancer, osteomyelitis, a resurrected dead kidney, car-train accident, double surgery and an opened kidney block. Medical professionals have documented each of these miracles as beyond medical reason.

These are but a few of the miracles that have been confirmed by those who witnessed them. There are millions of other physical healings and powerful deliverances that could be shared...but there is an even more phenomenal miracle for humans to experience. It is the miracle of "rebirth".

Human Experiences, God's Revelation   ***Chapter Six***

Everyone associated with human behavior...including those of the mental health profession, sociology, family counseling, ministry and clinical research, admit to the *impossibility of instantaneous life conversions* that change the entire nature of a human being. Yet, this is precisely what has happened to untold millions of people in the last 2000 years.

It is a life-changing event referred to in the Bible as being "born again". This "born again" experience completely converts a person from their evil and rebellious nature to a life of righteousness, love and devotion to God. No human ability can perform such a remarkable change, even over a lifetime...yet the born again experience occurs *instantaneously*.

How? The "born again" experience is a spiritual conversion performed by God through His Holy Spirit. It is a Divine intervention in the life of a human being whereby our evil nature is removed and replaced by a new (Godly) nature. Here is one example.

Have you ever heard the song "Amazing Grace?" It is one of the world's most famous hymns. The author was a former slave-ship captain who found God's amazing grace. His name was John Newton. He was born in England in 1725.

Newton's mother died when he was seven years old. When he was ten, his father (a sea captain and devoted Christian) took him permanently aboard ship. At age seventeen John became rebellious toward his father's religious teachings

Human Experiences, God's Revelation   **Chapter Six**

and left the ship. Some English officers kidnapped him to their ship where he was chained in irons and whipped. He deserted their ship and ended up on a small island off West Africa where he lived for a short time among the slaves.

He was sold to a cruel native woman who took great joy in making him beg for food. After several years of trying to escape, he finally found a visiting slave ship, and before long John Newton was the slave ship's captain. His crew, however, mutinied and left him marooned on a desolate island.

During all this time John's father prayed for him without knowing of his whereabouts. A friend found John and returned him to England where John resumed his hedonistic life style. He soon again became involved in the slave trade.

At age twenty-three Newton almost perished at sea while transporting slaves. A violent storm lashed the vessel he captioned, putting it into serious peril. Water rushed into the hold and all appeared lost. At that moment Newton cried out to God for "Mercy! Mercy!"...the first time he had uttered a prayer since childhood. As desperate men often do, Newton promised that he would turn his life over to God if he was spared from the storm.

Immediately the sea grew calm, the ship righted itself and the ship's hold was water free. Newton cried out, "It's a miracle from the Lord!"

Human Experiences, God's Revelation **Chapter Six**

Newton turned his life over to the Lord as he promised. He left the slave trade and eventually became a very successful minister with a dynamic influence and message. One evening, while preparing a sermon about his conversion experience, he prayed for help "Lord, you know how I was lost and that you, dear Jesus, found me and saved me." Suddenly the words began to flow from his pen...

Amazing grace! How sweet the sound
That saved a wretch like me!
I once was lost, but now am found,
Was blind, but now I see.

Twas grace that taught my heart to fear,
And grace my fears relieved,
How precious did that grace appear,
The hour I first believed!

The instant, miraculous change of this man's life cannot be explained other than by Divine intervention. Only the power of God is capable of changing a hardened infidel and slave trader into a faithful follower of Christ. It was the rich mercy (amazing grace) of God that forgave, restored, pardoned and changed this hardened man...who had long tried to destroy the faith he now embraced.

Human Experiences, God's Revelation   **Chapter Six**

Do miracles happen? John Newton is but one example of countless millions who have experienced the life changing grace of a loving God who forgives everyone who sincerely seeks his mercy to become "born-again" children by His power.

Many of these born-again "children" have been cruelly persecuted, imprisoned and put to death for their testimony and faith in Christ...yet they were willing to suffer for the truth that they had personally experienced. Their instant, miraculous life change and their willingness to die in devotion to their Creator, supports the claim that these converts had a genuine experience of Divine intervention.

No human resolution or ambition has yet been found that can accomplish such a remarkable life-changing turn-around ... nor would millions of people be willing to die for something they had not experienced. These untold millions of "God's true children" are a powerful evidence that there is a God.

SUMMARY

God has and still reveals Himself to the human family through various true miracles. But do miraculous life-changing experiences and "divine healings" provide credible evidence to the existence of God? To researchers, they do...

Human Experiences, God's Revelation   **Chapter Six**

1.   Instant spiritual conversions and complete physical healings continue to amaze medical and mental health professionals by events that cannot be medically explained.

2.   The history of Christians, who experienced a miraculous life transformation and then willingly presented themselves as martyrs, is another statement of Divine intervention beyond human understanding to which people are willing to die for.

3.   Evil people, instantly "converted" to a new life where they no longer engaged in evil and illegal activities, are also on record. Experts in every field of human behavior all agree that human beings have no power within themselves to make such a dramatic and instantaneous conversion in their life, regardless of how many resolutions or pledges they make.

4.   It appears from the huge number of testimonies that a Divine Being, more powerful and wise than humans, has intervened throughout history...to change human nature, to heal, to deliver, and to provide other essentials as they were needed.

I've witnessed and experienced miracles myself. I've read credible documentation of miracles. I've known and talked with people who have experienced miracles. None of these can be scientifically explained by logic or reason. Everywhere we look, reality just keeps getting better and better.

The Makeup And Character Of God   *Chapter Seven*

God's Makeup
and
Character

If you keep your ear open long enough you'll hear someone ask a question about why God deals with our human family the way He does. The questions center around human suffering and they go something like this ...

"Can God be trusted when He allows so many bad things to happen in our world?"

"Why is there so much evil in the world...can't God stop it...if He is all knowing and all powerful?"

"If a loving God created the world, why are there so many natural disasters like earthquakes, floods, hurricanes, tornadoes and famines that hurt and kill people?"

"What about birth defects, disease, illness, death...why would a loving God let these things happen to His creation?"

"Does God really answer prayer or are we left on our own to deal with all our problems?"

The Makeup And Character Of God　　　*Chapter Seven*

In the next chapter we'll look at these questions, but before we do, let's reacquaint ourselves with who God is and the character of God as defined in the Bible...a character that has been consistently expressed throughout human history.

These Biblical disclosures of God are very important, for without them we would be lost and estranged from Him who has the answers to the true meaning of life. In no other literature, religious or otherwise, are we introduced to the real God.

God lives in a spiritual environment that our earthly human experiences cannot fully understand. The magnificence and supremacy of God are beyond human intellect, and only that which God has revealed to us in His word is vaguely comprehendible.

The Bible does, however, reveal everything we need to know about our Creator in order that we may enjoy a wholesome relationship with Him...now and for eternity. But the challenge of any student and teacher in studying the topic of God is to accept the simple revelation of God as the Bible reveals it to us.

Anything beyond what the Bible teaches is left to human speculation and superstition...that have, throughout history, led to erroneous and deceptive views about God.

SUMMARY OF HOW THE BIBLE
IDENTIFIES GOD

The Makeup And Character Of God   Chapter Seven

There is one God in all of the universe who has revealed Himself in three persons; The Father, The Son and The Holy Spirit. This one God, who is the Creator of all things, is a God who loves each and every member of His human creation and desires the very best for each and every one of us.

This one simple statement offers the essence of how God is revealed to us in the Bible. For a better understanding let's look first to the features of God's makeup...features that are far superior to those which we humans possess. Then we will look at God's character to answer the question, "Can God be trusted?"

GOD IS SELF EXISTENT

God was not created or born as you and I were. He has no life source or parent.

For many people this is a hard concept to grasp, since everything in our physical world begins with a parental seed that conveys life to the offspring. But as the Bible reveals, God has no beginning. He has always existed and He is the life source of everything else in existence.

111

The Makeup And Character Of God   *Chapter Seven*

The Bible begins with the revelation that, "In the beginning God..." No further explanation is given throughout scripture. God is self-existent with the power of life within Himself.

> "God that made the world and all things therein, seeing that he is Lord of heaven and earth, dwelleth not in temples made with hands; Neither is worshipped with men's hands, as though he needed any thing, seeing he giveth to all life, and breath, and all things;."
>
> Acts 17:24-25 (KJV)

GOD IS ETERNAL

God has always existed and He always will...no beginning or end.

The eternal nature of God is also difficult for the human mind to comprehend, since our existence is one of birth and death where, in a short life span, we search for a meaningful existence.

To comprehend a Divine Being who forever exists is beyond comparison with anything we understand. But if what science suggests to us is true, that the universe is millions of years old, then the eternal nature of the Creator is well documented every time we look into the sky.

The Makeup And Character Of God   *Chapter Seven*

"For therein is the righteousness of God revealed from faith to faith: as it is written, the just shall live by faith.

For the wrath of God is revealed from heaven against all ungodliness and unrighteousness of men, who hold the truth in unrighteousness; Because that which may be known of God is manifest in them; for God hath showed it unto them. For the invisible things of him from the creation of the world are clearly seen, being understood by the things that are made, even his eternal power and Godhead; so that they are without excuse: Because that, when they knew God, they glorified him not as God, neither were thankful; but became vain in their imaginations, and their foolish heart was darkened. Professing themselves to be wise, they became fools, And changed the glory of the uncorruptible God into an image made like to corruptible man, and to birds, and fourfooted beasts, and creeping things.."

Romans 1:17-23 (KJV)

GOD IS OMNIPRESENT

God has the ability to be everywhere at the same time. This also is difficult for our human minds to comprehend.

God inhabits the entire universe and is always close by. There is nowhere that God cannot be, and there is nowhere we can go to escape from His presence.

The Makeup And Character Of God　　　*Chapter Seven*

"Can any hide himself in secret places that I shall not see him? saith the LORD. Do not I fill heaven and earth? saith the LORD."　　　Jeremiah 23:24

"...that they should seek the Lord, if haply they might feel after him, and find him, though he be not far from every one of us: For in him we live, and move, and have our being; as certain also of your own poets have said, For we are also his offspring.."　　Acts 17:27-28

GOD IS OMNISCIENT

Not only does God have unlimited presence...He also possesses unlimited knowledge. He knows everything about the physical universe where we live and everything about the creatures that He has created. He understands all science, nature, energy, emotion and human need.

"Known unto God are all his works from the beginning of the world."　　　Acts 15:18

(words of Jesus)　"... for your Father knows what things you have need of before ye ask him."　　Matthew 6:8

" Neither is there any creature that is not manifest in his sight: but all things are naked and opened unto the eyes of him with whom we have to do."　　　Hebrews 4:13

114

The Makeup And Character Of God   *Chapter Seven*

GOD IS OMNIPOTENT

The completeness of God's makeup is defined by His unlimited abilities to do anything He so desires. God has total control over everything and there's nothing beyond His ability... even things that are beyond our understanding.

Those things that we view as miraculous are but ordinary events to the mind and power of the Almighty God. He is not limited by physical science, space, time or energy as we know it.

> (words of Jesus)..." With men this is impossible; but with God all things are possible.."   Matthew 19:26

> "Now unto him that is able to do exceeding abundantly above all that we ask or think, according to the power that worketh in us, unto him be glory..."   Ephesians 3:20

But, even though God can do anything...there are some things that God will not do.

God will not do something that is against His will nor would God do something that would be harmful to any of His creation. God will do only that which is in our best interest.

God alone knows how to use His great powers to provide those things that are good for us and which are within His will for our lives.

115

The Makeup And Character Of God   *Chapter Seven*

SUMMARY OF GOD'S MAKEUP

The previous discussion reveals the features of God's makeup as the Bible reveals them to us.

God is self-existent and eternal. He is the source of all life and will live forever. He is the one and only God in the entire universe, revealing Himself to our human family in three persons as the Father, Son and Holy Spirit.

God is all knowing. He is everywhere and He can do anything. His abilities are unlimited as He is capable of transcending space, time, energy and all science, as we understand them. There is nothing that God cannot do...except that which is against our best interest.

These are features of our Creator who desires a relationship with every member of the human family. Now, to the big question on the minds of many people...

"CAN GOD REALLY BE TRUSTED TO HELP ME?"

Knowing the makeup of God is one thing...that He is all-powerful and wise...but understanding how He uses His abilities in behalf of *one individual human being* is something else. From everything we know and have confirmed throughout human history, you apparently are very special to your Creator.

The Makeup And Character Of God   *Chapter Seven*

The question of God's character is vital to every human being ... seeing that we are totally dependent upon Him for our survival. God's character is what motivates His actions...and His actions are what determine our total welfare and future.

Whether or not God can be trusted is revealed in His character. Centuries of false speculation regarding God's true character have created confusion, delusion and disappointment ...leading people to question "why?" ... "Why did God allow that to happen" or "Why hasn't God answered my prayer"?

Understanding the true character of God resolves the "why" questions once and for all. The summary of His character reveals this..."God simply can do nothing wrong or that is harmful in any way to His creation". The motives behind all of God's actions are those where our absolute, best interest is His supreme will. Ethical purity and moral perfection stand tall as traits of our Creator's character.

THE FIRST DESCRIPTIONS OF GOD'S CHARACTER
ARE
COMPASSION, MERCY AND GRACE

The English word "grace", used in the Bible, comes from the Greek word "charis" meaning "unmerited favor". It means "the receiving of something that we don't deserve"...and who doesn't need that from time to time. Here's how it works...

117

The Makeup And Character Of God   *Chapter Seven*

First...the problem. It was our choice to rebel against God to become sinners. Every human being has done that. God didn't force sin on us...we jumped into its bed by ourselves.

Second...the repercussion. Because of sin God moved out of our lives...leaving us to deal with sin's fury all alone. He will have nothing to do with sin in any form or fashion.

Third...the tragic results. Look at today's horrible headlines. Mankind is a mess and we can't do anything about it. We have no power to overcome sin's power. Sin is having a hey-day at the expense of our human family.

Fourth...the hope. All is not lost. God knows all about the situation...and being who He is, God feels compassion toward us even though we are rebellious sinners who have gone against His will. He isn't laughing at our tragedies...He grieves with our pain and suffering.

Fifth...getting something we don't deserve. God knows that we are entrapped with a power of sin far greater than we are able to control...and He is ready to do something about it... when we are ready to allow Him to do it. Here is where grace and mercy come in.

Even though we are the ones at fault...it is God who is extending a hand of forgiveness and deliverance from our sins... even though none of us deserve it. God is compassionate, merciful and full of grace. Someone with that quality of character can definitely be trusted.

118

The Makeup And Character Of God   *Chapter Seven*

"For thou, Lord, art good, and ready to forgive; and plenteous in mercy unto all them that call upon thee."

Psalms 86:5

"Let us therefore come boldly unto the throne of grace, that we may obtain mercy, and find grace to help in time of need."   Hebrews 4:16

GOD IS LOVE

Probably the most quoted scripture in all the Bible is ...

"For God so loved the world, that he gave his only begotten Son, that whosoever believes in him should not perish, but have everlasting life."   John 3:16

Love is one of those words overused and misused. The Greeks had three different terms for it...Agape, Eros and Phileo. "Eros" love is sexual love. We hear that one used a lot, but *eros* is never mentioned in the Bible. "Phileo" is friendship love... something like how brothers and sisters love each other.

"Agape" is "Godly love"...the kind of love God has... true, genuine, sacrificial love. The love of God is pure and inclusive. No human being on earth is excluded from God's love...even though each and every one of us has failed Him.

119

The Makeup And Character Of God   *Chapter Seven*

This kind of love is difficult for most human beings to fully understand. It offers healing rather than retribution... reconciliation rather than revenge.

God loves those who have turned their backs on him and He aggressively seeks to reconcile them to Himself. His love is so great that He sacrificed His only begotten Son so that the rebellious sinful human family could be forgiven.

God loves us even when we have shown, by our disobedience, that we did not love Him. Someone with that quality of character can definitely be trusted.

"Beloved, let us love one another: for love is of God; and every one that loveth is born of God, and knoweth God. He that loveth not knoweth not God; for God is love. In this was manifested the love of God toward us, because that God sent his only begotten Son into the world, that we might live through him. Herein is love, not that we loved God, but that he loved us, and sent his Son to be the propitiation for our sins. Beloved, if God so loved us, we ought also to love one another. No man hath seen God at any time. If we love one another, God dwelleth in us, and his love is perfected in us.

1 John 4:7-12

GOD IS IMPARTIAL

The Makeup And Character Of God   **Chapter Seven**

Another feature of God's character is that He makes no distinction between one person and another. Every human being is equally valuable in His sight...and what God is willing to do for one...He is willing to do for everyone.

God's love and mercy are extended to anyone who accepts them. Every human being has the assurance that we will be equally treated. The needs of one person are as urgent to God as the needs of anyone. Someone with that quality of character can definitely be trusted.

"But in every nation he that feareth him, and worketh righteousness, is accepted with him." Acts 10:35 (KJV)

GOD IS PATIENT

God has a "long mind"...which means that He is not quick to condemn or judge even those who have rebelled and turned from Him. Instead, God patiently waits for His human creation to return to His fellowship. Someone with that quality of character can definitely be trusted.

Bless the LORD, O my soul: and all that is within me, bless his holy name. Bless the LORD, O my soul, and forget not all his benefits: Who forgiveth all thine iniquities; who healeth all thy diseases; Who redeemeth

The Makeup And Character Of God　　　　　*Chapter Seven*

thy life from destruction; who crowneth thee with lovingkindness and tender mercies; Who satisfieth thy mouth with good things; so that thy youth is renewed like the eagle's. The LORD executeth righteousness and judgment for all that are oppressed. He made known his ways unto Moses, his acts unto the children of Israel. The LORD is merciful and gracious, slow to anger, and plenteous in mercy. He will not always chide: neither will he keep his anger for ever. He hath not dealt with us after our sins; nor rewarded us according to our iniquities. For as the heaven is high above the earth, so great is his mercy toward them that fear him. As far as the east is from the west, so far hath he removed our transgressions from us. Like as a father pitieth his children, so the LORD pitieth them that fear him.　　　Psalms 103:1-13

GOD IS GOOD

God's goodness is revealed in His intentions and efforts toward our human family. Everything He does is for our greatest well-being. He can be trusted to treat every member of our human family with the highest level of moral integrity and fairness. His motives are honorable and honest.

Nothing in God's character or in the history of His dealings with our human family would suggest anything about God other than perfect righteousness and trustworthiness.

122

The Makeup And Character Of God   *Chapter Seven*

In every act of God we are introduced to the purest and most excellent of virtues. Someone with that quality of character can definitely be trusted.

"O taste and see that the LORD is good: blessed is the man that trusteth in him."   Psalms 34:8

"If ye then, being evil, know how to give good gifts unto your children, how much more shall your Father which is in heaven give good things to them that ask him?"
                    (words of Jesus)   Matthew 7:11

GOD IS JUST

This is a characteristic of God that confuses many people. God is a judge who measures out true justice on good and evil alike.

True justice involves both reward and punishment. God rewards those who are good and punishes those who are evil. In His court of law…justice is fair, impartial and certain.

The question often heard is, "Would a loving and kind God really send someone to an everlasting punishment in hell?"

The answer is no, God would never send someone to an everlasting punishment…but He has allowed untold numbers to go there through their own choice.

123

The Makeup And Character Of God　　　*Chapter Seven*

True justice demands both reward and punishment. Anything less would undermine the integrity and authority of the Judge. Most human beings relate to the reward side of justice, but have difficulty accepting the punishment.

> "The LORD is in his holy temple, the LORD'S throne is in heaven: his eyes behold, his eyelids try, the children of men. The LORD trieth the righteous: but the wicked and him that loveth violence his soul hateth. Upon the wicked he shall rain snares, fire and brimstone, and an horrible tempest: this shall be the portion of their cup. For the righteous LORD loveth righteousness; his countenance doth behold the upright."　　　Psalms 11:4-7 (KJV)

> "And as it is appointed unto men once to die, but after this the judgment:"　　　Hebrews 9:27

The word "hate" used in the above scripture should not be misinterpreted with the way we use the word in our modern language. It is a word translated from the Hebrew that means "an enemy or foe".

In other words, God defines those who continually engage in wickedness and violence to be His foes or enemies. God loves their souls, but this does not mean that God will condone, endorse or overlook their continual evil rebellion.

124

The Makeup And Character Of God   **Chapter Seven**

God is our only eternal judge and His judgments are just. He looks upon the heart and actions of all people to determine our eternal outcome. The actions of the sinner provoke anger and retribution from the Lord while the righteous are accepted and rewarded. The choice is left to each one of us...shall I remain a rebellious sinner...or shall I seek the Lord with all my heart?

God's judgments cannot be compared with human justice, for His standards are far superior to those of our human courts where true justice is often repressed. While humans appear more lenient and hesitant to punish the wicked, God is not so lenient.

This is a disturbing reality for those who do not understand the implications of true justice. To dismiss the arrogant and rebellious sinner, who continually mocks His law and authority, would discredit God's integrity and character. His authority is defined and maintained by the fair administration of justice...that includes certain punishment to the sinner.

There is no plea-bargaining in God's court. To allow the sinner a reprieve would undermine God's authority. Even so, God constantly seeks to forgive the sinner...if they desire His forgiveness to turn away from their sins. But if not, God is fair and impartial...and certain to administer His true justice on every human being. There is an appointed date for each of us to stand before the judgment seat of God.

125

The Makeup And Character Of God   *Chapter Seven*

"For we know him that hath said, Vengeance belongeth
unto me, I will recompense, saith the Lord. And again,
The Lord shall judge his people. It is a fearful thing to fall
into the hands of the living God."   Hebrews 10:30-31

GOD IS HOLY AND TRUTHFUL

The Bible reveals God to be "holy", a word taken from
the Greek word, "hagios", meaning "sacred" or "blameless". It
defines God as faultless, innocent and pure...undefiled in any
way.

God is further identified to be "truthful", from the
Hebrew word, "emuwnah", and the Greek, "aletheia". Both
words define God as not only factual and accurate in all that He
says and does...but also identifies Him to be unwavering and
consistent. His "truths" are eternally accurate and without
error...and His stand for "truth" is constant and unwavering.
God knows what is truth...He will always do and tell the
truth...and God will never be changed or swayed from truth.

"The LORD is righteous in all his ways, and holy in all
his works.   Psalms 145:17 (KJV)

"For the word of the LORD is right; and all his works are
done in truth."   Psalms33:4

The Makeup And Character Of God   **Chapter Seven**

God, who is innocent and undefiled in every way, can forever be relied upon to treat His creation with truth and integrity. He can be relied upon to be truthful in all that He says and does. His works and decisions are beyond reproach.

Someone with that quality of character can definitely be trusted.

GOD IS COMPLETE AND PERFECT

Nothing is missing with God. He is whole and complete... nothing more can be added to His makeup or character.

"Perfection" and "holiness" are terms with separate meanings. The term "holiness" defines faultlessness or purity... while "perfection" defines totality or completeness. God possesses both.

> "He is the Rock, his work is perfect: for all his ways are judgment...a God of truth and without iniquity, just and right is he."   Deuteronomy 32:4

God is both without fault and complete in His character, in His abilities, and in His involvement with the human family.

Someone with that quality of character can definitely be trusted.

127

The Makeup And Character Of God   *Chapter Seven*

GOD IS WISE

God not only has unlimited knowledge...He also possesses the wisdom of how to use His knowledge to its greatest potential. Knowledge without wisdom is of little value ...as most of us have realized at some time or another in our life.

Knowledge alone does not solve problems. Wisdom is the key that unlocks the power of knowledge. Without wisdom, knowledge lies dormant. God possesses both knowledge and the wisdom of how to use His unlimited knowledge.

> "Glory and honor to God forever and ever. He is the King of the ages, the unseen one who never dies; he alone is God, and full of wisdom."   1 Timothy 1:17

God does not abuse or misuse His infinite knowledge. He knows how to capitalize on His knowledge to its greatest potential... with our best interests always in mind. Someone with that quality of character can definitely be trusted.

GOD IS SOVEREIGN

God is the most powerful Being in the entire universe. He can do all things...and He is above all things. (complete sovereignty). There is no greater authority than God. He rules over all and His throne is established forever in Heaven.

128

The Makeup And Character Of God   *Chapter Seven*

"Thou art worthy, O Lord, to receive glory and honor and power: for thou hast created all things, and for thy pleasure they are and were created.   Revelation 4:11 (KJV)

God has sovereign authority (power) over all creation. Nothing exists or functions beyond the will of God. All things were created by Him and for Him. Mankind is but a part of that creation...to respect God's other life creations and environment.

"And every creature which is in heaven, and on the earth, and under the earth, and such as are in the sea, and all that are in them, heard I saying, Blessing, and honour, and glory, and power, be unto him that sitteth upon the throne, and unto the Lamb for ever and ever. And after these things I heard a great voice of much people in heaven, saying, Alleluia; Salvation, and glory, and honour, and power, unto the Lord our God"

Revelation 5:13 and 19:1 (KJV)

God has sovereign authority (power) over heaven and earth...and over all creatures therein. There are no limits to God's authority ...spiritual or physical. All are subordinate to God. God's sovereign authority has never been relinquished to any other creature or being. He retains all authoritative power now and forever. There is none in all the universe equal to Him. Someone with that quality of character can definitely be trusted.

129

The Makeup And Character Of God　　　*Chapter Seven*

GOD IS FAITHFUL

God can be relied upon to do all that He has promised. He never fails on any of His promises...including the promise to answer our prayers.

God has promised us a "more abundant life"...a life of peace and joy. He has promised to provide for our physical and spiritual needs. God has promised to guide us into all truth and to protect us from our spiritual enemies. God has promised to never forsake His people...that He will be with us in every situation and circumstance. No one in all of human history can correctly say that God has ever failed them.

Although God has made promises to our human family...every promise comes with a condition. God has promised to answer our prayers...but God will not answer foolish prayers that are against His will or that are harmful to us in some way. God cares what happens to us and He is wise enough to know the difference between a harmful prayer and a constructive prayer. Foolish children sometimes want foolish things. A wise parent knows when to withhold a child's request for the child's benefit.

" And they that know thy name will put their trust in thee: for thou, LORD, hast not forsaken them that seek thee."　　　　　　　　　　　　　　　Psalms 9:10 (KJV)

The Makeup And Character Of God   Chapter Seven

" For ever, O LORD, thy word is settled in heaven. Thy
faithfulness is unto all generations: thou hast established
the earth, and it abideth. They continue this day
according to thine ordinances: for all are thy servants.."

Psalms 119:89 (KJV)

"If we confess our sins, he is faithful and just to forgive
us our sins, and to cleanse us from all unrighteousness."

1 John 1:9

The faithfulness of God does not mean that He is our
servant to snap at attention when we call. He knows what we
have need of...even before we ask. He is watching over us and
will not forsake those who trust in Him. God is a wise Father
who is faithful to the total welfare and safety of His children.
Someone with that quality of character can definitely be trusted.

GOD IS A GOD OF GLORY

The Greek word, "doxa", from where we translate our
English word, "glory", means dignity or honor. God possesses
both. There is none like Him in the spiritual or physical worlds.

Giving glory (praise/worship) to a glorious (dignified)
God is a natural act of those who know Him. He alone is
affirmed to be of such honor as to deserve the highest reverence
and deepest worship.

The Makeup And Character Of God   Chapter Seven

"Now unto him that is able to keep you from falling, and to present you faultless before the presence of his glory with exceeding joy...To the only wise God our Savior, be glory and majesty, dominion and power, both now and for ever. Amen."   Jude 1: 24-25

The God revealed to us in the Bible...as well as in our human experiences...has earned the respect and praise of His creation. He is respected, not only because of His lofty position, but also because of His lofty and unblemished character. God's dignity as a righteous and perfect Creator of the universe is worthy of our deepest respect and reverence. There is none like Him.

Someone with that quality of character can definitely be trusted.

GOD IS A JEALOUS GOD

This is a character trait of God that some people may find confusing. God demands complete allegiance and reverence. There is no room for worship or allegiance to any other gods beyond Him. His jealousy in that regard is most intense. But the jealousy of God should not be compared with the jealousy of human beings... which is where many people become confused.

The Makeup And Character Of God   *Chapter Seven*

There are two Hebrew words from where our English word, "jealous" is translated in the Bible. The first, "qanna ", simply means "jealous"...while "qana" has a more prime root meaning ... "to be or to make <u>zealous</u>". There is an important distinction between the two terms.

"Gana" is the kind of jealousy (in a bad sense) that is envious of another...which in turn provokes an unrealistic, excessive zeal. This is the kind of jealousy that human beings exhibit when we are intimidated or envious of others. Such jealousy provokes <u>zealous</u> responses that puts pressures and demands...even emotional and physical harm...on the victim of our jealousy.

The "ganna" jealousy of God is different. God is not intimated, threatened or envious of any creature...nor is He engaged in zealous attempts to provoke or pressure someone into submission. His jealousy, that demands total allegiance to Himself, is inspired by His lofty position of honor, dignity and integrity. God alone deserves total honor and worship... and to demand any less from His creation would not fit the sublime nature of His character.

Nothing can become a substitute for God without provoking the jealousy of God. The gods of religion, education, science, power and wealth...that we have resolved to be our life's securities... have distracted mankind from allegiance and trust of the real God. These things create "Godly jealousy".

133

The Makeup And Character Of God   Chapter Seven

"You shall not bow down to any images nor worship them in any way, for I am the Lord your God. I am a jealous God, and I will bring the curse of a father's sins upon even the third and fourth generation of the children of those who hate me; but I will show kindness to a thousand generations of those who love me and keep my commandments."   Deuteronomy 5:9-10

"For thou shalt worship no other god: for the LORD, whose name is Jealous, is a jealous God:" Exodus 34:14

Someone with the dignity and self-respect...to not allow any other thing to be honored above Him...is someone who can be trusted to also respect our human dignity...as His creation.

GOD IS IMMUTABLE (UNCHANGING)

God never changes...He will forever be as He always has been. He is the same yesterday, today and forever...even when times and circumstances change.

Human history on earth has undergone drastic reconstruction throughout the ages...yet, despite the changing status of our cultures and moral depravation, the character and will of God are still intact. His relationship with our human family has remained stable and certain...even in the unstable and uncertain times in which we currently live.

134

The Makeup And Character Of God   *Chapter Seven*

The same God that we read about in the Old Testament times and in the New Testament times is the same One who we relate to today. Time and circumstance do not change God.

"For I am the LORD, I change not."   Malachi 3:6

" Every good gift and every perfect gift is from above, and cometh down from the Father of lights, with whom is no variableness, neither shadow of turning."   James 1:17

God's stability and unchanging character is the only foundation on which our human existence has any meaning. He is the solid rock on which we stand...all other ground is sinking sand. Someone with that quality of character can definitely be trusted.

SUMMARY OF WHO GOD IS

The Biblical revelation of God has been confirmed by human experience. God is a self-existent spirit who will forever exist...and who is all knowing, all powerful and everywhere present. This one eternal God is a God of love and compassion ...patient and merciful to every person who allows Him to be a part of their life. He judges all people alike with proper justice ...to reward good and punish evil.

The Makeup And Character Of God   **Chapter Seven**

God does everything right...there is no error in Him. God never makes mistakes and is wise to know how to use His perfect knowledge of all things. He is a faithful God who will never fail on any of His promises...but He is a jealous God who demands complete reverence and allegiance.

God never changes, even in a world that seems to change constantly. He is the solid rock on which life is stabilized. He is always there to meet our needs in every way.

He is a merciful God who can be trusted...and because of that, our human family can be assured of a good life here on earth while possessing the hope of life after death. This assurance and hope comes to those who humbly submit to Him as the Sovereign Creator.

Someone with the character and qualities that God possesses can definitely be trusted.

Sadly, and tragically, mankind as a whole has desired to exist without our Creator. Our human failures and calamities have proven how terrible that choice has been. Even so, with that said, there still is the question in the minds of many people ...Why does a good God allow bad things to happen to good people? In the next chapter we share the answers to that question.

Everywhere we look, reality just keeps getting better and better.

Why Does God Allow Bad Things?   **Chapter Eight**

Why Does God Allow Bad Things To Happen... And Why Doesn't He Do Something To Fix The Problems?

One of the leading questions that professional counselors hear in regards to God is ... "If God is so good, why is there so much evil and pain and suffering in the world? For some, this is a question born from confusion, while for others it is a question that smirks or challenges the existence of God and His integrity. Either way, it is a question that deserves an honest answer.

There are a lot of things going wrong in the world. That's for sure. We humans get hit with sickness, disease, birth defects, natural disasters, crime, war, etc., etc., etc. Then we die. So, who's to blame?

The first reaction of many people is to blame God...but is that fair...or realistic? Is God really the author of all the pain and suffering in the world, or should we look elsewhere? Sure, God could make the world a paradise if He wanted to...or can He? Let's look at the reality of our situation.

137

Why Does God Allow Bad Things?   **Chapter Eight**

There are three possibilities for human suffering. One is God. Another is ourselves. The third is an evil spirit (or spirits) who has control over human life.

Eliminating dumb, bad luck as the culprit...where bad stuff just happens by itself...we are confronted with the reality that all human suffering is caused by someone.

THE CERTAIN ANSWER

According to the Bible, God is a good God...and everything He created was good, including human beings. By the word "good", it is meant... "perfect"..."without fault".

There was, at one time, no fault with anything that God had created. All things were under God's supervision, including nature and all living creatures. Everything performed the way it was supposed to perform. The world was in perfect harmony and all creatures were disciplined to the authority of the Creator... who made everything work smoothly. But then tragedy struck!

Of all the creatures that God made, there was only one created with the "power of choice". That creature was a human being, who has the power to make conscious decisions, unlike the animal kingdom that functions on instinct. Mankind, alone, has the ability to think, logic things out, make plans and develop wisdom. We are not robots that live and function at the push of a button. We have a will and a brain by which we make decisions.

Why Does God Allow Bad Things?   *Chapter Eight*

Our Creator has given human beings the powerful gift of "choice". But with this "power of choice" comes a great burden of responsibility. Our "intellectual power" and "freedom of choice" are both a great blessing and an enigma for humans.

We have the power to choose who we serve and how we want to act. We can choose to serve the Creator who made us, or we can choose to serve another "god" as replacement. The tragedy of history is that humanity has chosen to serve other "gods"... including ourselves! The result of our rebellion against our Creator has been a variety of human miseries!

Humans cannot blame God for our problems, nor can we totally blame the devil. But one might ask... "Can't God intervene to help us solve our problems?"   The answer is ...He already has ... the world just isn't listening.

I've learned from years of experience in human behavior, that many people deal with their problems in one of two ways. They either avoid or deny that a problem exists...or they try to blame their problem on someone else.

We're not going to take either of those approaches in this writing...even though the truth is sometimes difficult to swallow. So, here's the bottom line ... all human problems are caused by human beings. But we don't want to hear that, do we?

Let's back up and begin at the beginning. Human problems all began with Adam and Eve in the Garden of Eden. You know the story.

139

Why Does God Allow Bad Things?   **Chapter Eight**

Adam and Eve were enjoying the great life where all their wishes and wants were totally supplied. The only problem was...they were dependent on their Creator to supply all the good stuff they wanted. Adam and Eve needed God for their existence. Besides that, God made all the rules.

With the help of a tempter, Adam and Eve decided that they could live without the influence or authority of their Creator. They could make it on their own. They listened to the tempter who suggested... "You will be as gods".

So, Adam and Even became rebellious "sinners" ... rejecting and denying the authority and laws of God. The suggestion that they could be their own "gods" ... that they did not need their Creator...was the lure that hooked Adam and Eve from the safety of God's oversight and provisional care...to propel them into a world where they could be the boss. And ever since then, mankind thinks he or she has been his or her own "boss". No wonder the world is in such a mess.

The consequence of their rebellion was that God left Adam and Eve alone to do their thing. He expelled them from His presence in the Garden of Eden, sending them out into the world to become their own gods. Adam and Eve were now on their own...just the way they wanted it.

Shortly thereafter, one of their sons murdered his brother ... and mankind has been killing and abusing one another ever since. But that's just the beginning.

Why Does God Allow Bad Things?   **Chapter Eight**

The rebellious, sinful nature of Adam and Eve has been passed down to the human race. Every one of us has been "born in sin".... which means...we have inherited the rebellious nature of our forefathers. And, as history confirms, that is certainly nothing to shout about.

Mankind continues to fail miserably...while God allows us to be our own boss. It appears that we humans can create problems very well, but when it comes to solving problems... mankind has a lousy track record. But we don't want to hear that, do we? Surely, man cannot be blamed for all his troubles.

Well, in a way we are and in a way we are not. There happens to be an evil spirit who still paints a pretty picture for our human family. This evil spirit, referred to in the Bible as satan (devil), is an enemy who desires total control of our life. His suggestions are the same as those in the beginning...that we can be our own god without having to bow to the authority of a Higher Divine Being.

Tragically, our human family has fallen prey to those suggestions, just as Adam and Eve did...but it doesn't have to be that way. Humans still possess the gift and "power of choice" ...to decide if we want to coddle satan's tempting indulgences.

Here is something many people do not understand ... man (woman) is not his (her) own boss. The Bible teaches that mankind is under the control of the spiritual world ... that there is no such thing as being independent.

141

Why Does God Allow Bad Things?   **Chapter Eight**

In other words, man is not god...and we're not in control of the situation. That makes sense when we remind ourselves that we are, after all, only creatures and not creators.

Human beings are either under the power and control of a spiritual God, or under the power and control of a spiritual "satan" ... the same evil spirit who was the tempter of Adam and Eve. There is no middle ground...even though the arrogance of human thinking tries to suggest otherwise.

The only power that mankind has, is our "power of choice". We can choose who we want as our God ... the loving heavenly Father or the cruel devil of the underworld. There are no other alternatives. In other words, man cannot avoid the spiritual world to live beyond its spiritual influence.

Some philosophers and intellectuals try to convince us that man is in control of his own ship...that we are self-born, self-sufficient and self-ruled. In other words...we are god. But, according to human history, this logic doesn't compute with reality.

It is revealed in the Bible and confirmed by human life on earth that a righteous God or an unrighteous demon controls human beings. Whichever spirit has control of our life will dictate the way we act and the way we think. An unrighteous (evil) spirit will lead us to unrighteous (evil) deeds while a righteous (good) spirit will lead us to deeds of righteousness (goodness). This is a powerful truth...not just a cute Bible story.

142

Why Does God Allow Bad Things?   *Chapter Eight*

The inner evil nature that influences our human activity and our relationships is referred to as "sin". Sin is two things ... it is rebellion against God and it is an inner evil "power" that compels us to action. It is this power of sin within human nature that has dictated man's history over the centuries.

Sin (not God) is the cause of all evil, pain and suffering. Sin is man's entire problem. If sin were totally abolished, then every problem on earth would immediately be resolved. That is what the Bible teaches...and how simple life really is.

The consequences of sin are evident all around us. Mankind is suffering. Sin affects the way we treat one another as human beings...and it also affects how we treat the natural environment that we depend upon for our human survival.

The list of how humans disrespect and treat one another is very long. Criminal activity, violent dominance, oppression, apathy, disrespect... just for starters. We are so consumed with self-rights, self-preservation and self-supremacy...that we will utterly destroy another living human being for self interests. Its all about this god we call "self".

Why have we destroyed one another throughout history? Is God at fault? Is He making us do it? Why does man blame God for man's choices? Humans cause human problems.

BIRTH DEFECTS, DISEASE,
ILLNESS, PREMATURE DEATH

Why Does God Allow Bad Things?   *Chapter Eight*

What about those things over which we have no control? Who is to blame for all the sickness and disease that humans are suffering? Is God punishing the human family? Surely, we don't purposely bring bad things like birth defects or cancer on ourselves, do we?

I guess you would have to say that I am an expert observer on this topic. Most of my adult life I have dealt with cancer somewhere on my body. I've had non-threatening (carcinoma) skin cancer and potentially fatal (melanoma) skin cancer. I've also had kidney cancer and colon cancer...either of which could have made my wife a widow. Besides the 50-75 minor cancer surgeries, I've also had three major cancer operations and chemotherapy. My health insurance provider doesn't like me very well.

So, the question one might ask is... "Why does Ken, or anyone else, have to suffer from some debilitating disease? Is Ken being punished? What did Ken do to deserve all this bad stuff? And why do some kids start out in life with a severe birth defect? Is the child being punished before it's ever born?

The answer is obvious to myself and to those in the scientific medical professions. I either breathed contaminated air, drank polluted water, or ate something in my diet that my body was not designed to ingest. This explanation for my illnesses can also be carried over to every illness on the planet, including those we call contagious...as well as birth defects.

144

Why Does God Allow Bad Things? **Chapter Eight**

All birth defects can be linked to the parental seeds. The fetus didn't do it on its own. Apparently, mom or dad passed along some defect as the result of a corrupted world.

What this all says is...our physical environment no longer is friendly to human life and we are suffering a lot of diseases and defects because of it. So, the question is... "Who is at fault for the breakdown of the environment?"

God made everything perfect. Man became god. We took charge of God's environment and we misused it. Mankind is to blame for our diseases, afflictions, defects and premature deaths. We corrupted God's environment for self-interests.

God is not at fault for man's evils, man's diseases or troubles. We did it to ourselves by listening to the tempter, who suggested that we could be our own gods to live beyond the protection, provision and guidance of a Heavenly Father ... who knows more about what we need than we do.

Life is that basic, even though we do not want to admit to ourselves that we are the cause of all our pain and grief. Our rebellion against our Creator (sin) has brought on all our problems. Our physical problems, social problems, mental problems and spiritual problems can all be traced back to man's rebellion against God. Sin has caused deception, shame and guilt. Sin is the cause of our wounds, our sickness, our miseries. Every human misery can be traced back to sin (our disrespect and rebellion against God's authority).

145

Why Does God Allow Bad Things?   *Chapter Eight*

That is the tragic reality of human life in a nutshell. But, fortunately, there is hope.

My particular illnesses are minor compared to what other people have suffered. I live in a world where sinful people have affected the environment on which I depend for my survival. My body had a specific gene that could not adjust to some environmental corruption. I got sick. Could God have spared me? Yes, only by removing me from the corrupted world. Could God have healed me? He did. I survive because of His mercy...but had God elected to call me home to His reward, that would have been OK also.

The apostle, Paul, suffered many afflictions and finally gave his life as a martyr for his testimony of Christ. Could God have spared him? He did! God called Paul home to eternal glory. Paul put life into perspective this way.... "If in this world only we have hope, we are of all men most miserable."

If that sounds fatalistic, consider these words, also from Paul... "I know in whom I have believed and I am persuaded that He is able to take care of that which I commit unto Him."

Paul understood that the world was inhabited by evil men with evil intentions who did evil things to other people ... good and evil alike. Will the world ever be the paradise that God created in the beginning? No. But there is another paradise waiting for those who love God enough that they want to live with Him for eternity. It's referred to it as heaven.

Why Does God Allow Bad Things?   **Chapter Eight**

While we live on earth we will experience problems that have been created by man's rebellion against his Creator. But even though we all experience problems, those who have placed their trust in God know this ... "We are more than conquerors through Him who loves us."

Here are a couple verses from the Bible that helps to explain why I not only believe in God ... but why I also place my total trust in Him ...

"The Spirit itself beareth witness with our spirit, that we are the children of God: And if children, then heirs; heirs of God, and joint-heirs with Christ; if so be that we suffer with him, that we may be also glorified together. For I reckon that the sufferings of this present time are not worthy to be compared with the glory which shall be revealed in us."

Romans 8:16-18

"And we know that all things work together for good to them that love God, to them who are the called according to his purpose"   Romans 8:28

"Who shall separate us from the love of Christ? shall tribulation, or distress, or persecution, or famine, or nakedness, or peril, or sword?...Nay, in all these things we are more than conquerors through him that loved us. For I am persuaded, that neither death, nor life, nor angels, nor

147

Why Does God Allow Bad Things?   *Chapter Eight*

principalities, nor powers, nor things present, nor things to come, Nor height, nor depth, nor any other creature, shall be able to separate us from the love of God, which is in Christ Jesus our Lord."   Romans 8:35-39

Good people live in an evil world. Sometimes that evil overwhelms them. Good people get sick and die. Good people suffer. Sincere Christians have been martyred for their faith. So, where is God?

God is forever watching. Sometimes He delivers and sometimes He doesn't. Sometimes He heals and sometimes He allows a sickness unto death. But even when God doesn't deliver or heal... the end of this life is only a step to the next life where evil no longer exists.

The reality of life is this…there is no lasting happiness on earth. Something painful is coming...possibly sickness, suffering and pain ... but for sure, death. And there's nothing we can do about that...other than to accept and prepare for it. For those who trust in God ... life is good no matter what happens… especially when you know the ending.

Everywhere we look, reality just keeps getting better and better.

Does God Care What Happens To Me?   *Chapter Nine*

Does God Really Care What Happens To Me... Personally

Another question on many people's minds is in regards to God's involvement in their personal lives. It is a question that asks if the God of the universe is available only to the human family at large...or are we important enough as individuals for God to become personally involved?

Although we may acknowledge God as the Bible defines Him (Supreme Deity), many people find it difficult to identify God as a personal friend who relates to human beings on an individual level...to become involved in our everyday life.

DOES GOD REALLY CARE WHAT HAPPENS TO ME ENOUGH TO GET INVOLVED?

God is more than just a spectator in the affairs of our human family...He is an enthusiastic participant. The Bible reveals God's involvement in our individual lives by the five roles that God has assumed for Himself in our behalf. They are the roles of Father, Guide, Preserver, Provider and Savior.

149

Does God Care What Happens To Me?   *Chapter Nine*

THE ROLE AND WORK OF GOD
AS FATHER

The Bible's definition of God as our Heavenly Father reveals an intimate relationship between a sovereign Creator and His creation. The role of fatherhood that God has chosen for Himself is one of devotion and responsibility...that assumes oversight for the welfare of a tender, vulnerable child...a role we also demand of human fathers. A devoted and responsible father fulfills certain obligations in behalf of his children...

1.   He provides for their basic essentials of survival that include food, clothing and shelter....as well as other basics.

2.   He protects his children from anything that could be harmful or destructive to them.

3.   He helps in the development of his children through love, encouragement, training and discipline.

In other words, the obligation of fatherhood is to assure the total welfare and growth of his offspring. This is the role that God has assumed as a spiritual Father to His spiritual children.

Does God Care What Happens To Me?   *Chapter Nine*

As a spiritual Father, God provides for all His children's spiritual needs.

As a spiritual Father, God protects us from our spiritual enemies.

As a spiritual Father, God also helps to develop our spiritual life...and our relationship with Him.

Our Heavenly Father has an interest in the total welfare of His children and He is capable of fulfilling His Fatherly role. Our success as God's spiritual children is assured. We shall be victorious both in this life and the life to come, because our Heavenly Father loves us and is capable to do whatever is necessary for our total welfare.

> "And I will be a Father unto you, and ye shall be my sons and daughters, saith the Lord Almighty."
>
> II Corinthians 6:18

> "If ye then, being evil, know how to give good gifts unto your children, how much more shall your Father which is in heaven give good things to them that ask him?"
>
> Matthew 7:11

The relationship between a spiritual father and spiritual child produces comfort and hope that can be found nowhere else in our human experience. The tender care of a Heavenly Father insures a life of peace, happiness and stability.

151

Does God Care What Happens To Me?   *Chapter Nine*

THE ROLE AND WORK OF GOD
AS GUIDE

The frightening thing about life is to not know where to turn for an answer. There are so many philosophies, so many religions, so many theories...so many contradictory opinions. Is there a true guide to lead us through the mire of human speculation and superstition...a guide to reality and hope?

Yes there is.

> "The meek will he guide in judgment: and the meek will he teach his way. All the paths of the LORD are mercy and truth unto such as keep his covenant and his testimonies."   Psalms 25:9-10

> (words of Jesus) "However, when He, the Spirit of truth, has come, He will guide you into all truth; for He will not speak on His own authority, but whatever He hears He will speak; and He will tell you things to come."
>   John 16:13

Some of the most intense and urgent questions that human beings ask themselves are fully resolved with the help of God... questions such as: Who am I? Why am I here? Where am I going? How am I going to get there? With the help of God, we are certain to find the right answers to all our questions.

152

Does God Care What Happens To Me? **Chapter Nine**

Life is not confusing or difficult when we know that we are not alone in our journey. God has promised to guide us all the way...

" And ye shall know the truth, and the truth shall make you free." John 8:32

"Let your conversation be without covetousness; and be content with such things as ye have: for he hath said, I will never leave thee, nor forsake thee. So that we may boldly say, The Lord is my helper, and I will not fear what man shall do unto me." Hebrews 13:5-6

THE ROLE AND WORK OF GOD
AS PRESERVER

Regardless of life's circumstance...there is help and there is hope. God preserves His people from all the difficulties and troubles of life. But that doesn't mean we will be removed from life where troubles exist.

The news reports constantly remind us of the danger and turmoil in our world. Even the best of life styles has the possibility of trouble in some way. September 11, 2001 was such an example. Life is very tentative, to say the least.

Does God Care What Happens To Me?   *Chapter Nine*

Crime, health and money concerns are only a part of the potential hazards of human life...not to mention the reality that we also battle spiritual enemies who desire to "kill, steal and destroy" our spiritual existence. The fragile human experience is one of potential danger from many seen and unseen sources.

Defending ourselves from life's hazards has become a top priority of this time in which we live. Who can protect us? Can our police, our political leaders, our scientists, our educators, or our health professionals guarantee a safe and secure life for us? Of course not! No one expects our social structures to resolve and preserve us from the world's evils.

But the Bible offers another alternative...trust in God and be sheltered from the effects of evil men and evil spirits.

God has promised to be a very present help in time of need...to guarantee that nothing will destroy us, no matter how difficult the troubles we may have to confront. God will never fail His people...regardless of what we must deal with in life. I've personally found that to be true.

But "preservation" and "elimination" are two different things. It would be nice to never have to deal with any problems or potential dangers...but God has not promised to eliminate the enemies of our life...only to protect us from them. To remove us from trouble would mean that we must be removed from the earth...for trouble will always exist as long as the earth survives.

In that light, Jesus prayed for His followers this way...

Does God Care What Happens To Me?   **Chapter Nine**

"I pray not that thou shouldest take them out of the world, but that thou shouldest keep them from the evil. They are not of the world, even as I am not of the world. "   John 17:15-16

God watches over and preserves His people in the midst of a tumultuous and violent world. He preserves His people from the effects of any harmful thing...war, crime, disease, etc. His people may have to deal with these issues...but never will God's people be overcome or consumed by them.

" Thou shalt keep them, O LORD, thou shalt preserve them from this generation for ever. The wicked walk on every side, when the vilest men are exalted. "

Psalms 12:7-8

"The LORD also will be a refuge for the oppressed, a refuge in times of trouble. And they that know thy name will put their trust in thee: for thou, LORD, hast not forsaken them that seek thee."   Psalms 9:9-10

"But the Lord is faithful, who shall stablish you, and keep you from evil."   2 Thessalonians 3:3

I've been there... and I can assure you, the peace of God in difficult times is a fortress that assures you... all is well!

155

Does God Care What Happens To Me?   *Chapter Nine*

THE ROLE AND WORK OF GOD
AS PROVIDER

Does mankind really need God? Is there any reason to pray? Have we advanced in our modern technology and scientific achievements to where we are capable of existing without the intrusion of God in our lives?

The answer to those questions is simple. When mankind learns how to bring rain where rain is needed...sunshine where warmth is urgent...and how to control the nature of seasons and manipulation of the wind...then man can say he has no need of God. Until then...we need God.

When mankind learns how to solve its world problems ...to change the hearts of evil men...to heal all pain and suffering...and to assure that there will be a tomorrow... then man can say he has no need of God. Until then...we need God.

The reality of life is...we are totally dependent upon that which our Creator provides. God still maintains His creation to provide for the essentials of human life. His blessings still provide the food we eat, the water we drink and the air we breathe. Without God's providential care, we are doomed to no longer exist.

To those who truly trust Him...God will provide all the essential needs of life...and more. There is no hunger or thirst to those who have faith in the loving care of their Creator.

156

Does God Care What Happens To Me?   *Chapter Nine*

"The LORD is my shepherd; I shall not want" Psalms 23:1

"I have been young, and now am old; yet have I not seen the righteous forsaken, nor his seed begging bread."

Psalms 37:25 TLB

"Behold the fowls of the air: for they sow not, neither do they reap, nor gather into barns; yet your heavenly Father feedeth them. Are ye not much better than they? Which of you by taking thought can add one cubit unto his stature? And why take ye thought for raiment? Consider the lilies of the field, how they grow; they toil not, neither do they spin: And yet I say unto you, That even Solomon in all his glory was not arrayed like one of these. Wherefore, if God so clothe the grass of the field, which to day is, and to morrow is cast into the oven, shall he not much more clothe you, O ye of little faith? Therefore take no thought, saying, What shall we eat? or, What shall we drink? or, Wherewithal shall we be clothed? (For after all these things do the Gentiles seek:) for your heavenly Father knoweth that ye have need of all these things. But seek ye first the kingdom of God, and his righteousness; and all these things shall be added unto you. Take therefore no thought for the morrow: for the morrow shall take thought for the things of itself. Sufficient unto the day is the evil thereof."   Matthew 6:26-34

Does God Care What Happens To Me?　　　　**Chapter Nine**

"But this I say, He which soweth sparingly shall reap also sparingly; and he which soweth bountifully shall reap also bountifully. Every man according as he purposeth in his heart, so let him give; not grudgingly, or of necessity: for God loveth a cheerful giver. And God is able to make all grace abound toward you; that ye, always having all sufficiency in all things, may abound to every good work: (As it is written, He hath dispersed abroad; he hath given to the poor: his righteousness remaineth for ever. Now he that ministereth seed to the sower both minister bread for your food, and multiply your seed sown, and increase the fruits of your righteousness;) Being enriched in every thing to all bountifulness, which causeth through us thanksgiving to God. For the administration of this service not only supplieth the want of the saints, but is abundant also by many thanksgivings unto God; Whiles by the experiment of this ministration they glorify God for your professed subjection unto the gospel of Christ, and for your liberal distribution unto them, and unto all men; And by their prayer for you, which long after you for the exceeding grace of God in you. Thanks be unto God for his unspeakable gift" (His Son)　　2 Corinthians 9:6-15

QUESTION... If God provides all the necessities for human survival, why is there so much hunger in the world? Why are there so many homeless people? Why must so many people have to struggle with life?

Does God Care What Happens To Me?   *Chapter Nine*

As we discussed previously, mankind has created problems for man. There are enough natural resources in our world that no one must go hungry or without shelter. God has provided plenty for everyone ... but man has become selfish ... to allow some to get rich while others remain poor. Its all out there ... all we have to do is share it equally with one another.

And, as for disease and illness...science is coming to understand that there are substances somewhere on our planet that will cure every disease of mankind. Some of those substances are now being used to help suffering humanity, while others are yet to be discovered.

Even though we have rebelled against our Creator, and by that rebellion we now suffer many afflictions and diseases... our God has lovingly provided cures somewhere in His providential nursery.

THE ROLE AND WORK OF GOD
AS OUR SAVIOR

The Bible teaches that mankind's only problem is our rebellion against God and His laws. That rebellion is referred to as "sin"...which is the cause of every human problem. War, crime, family troubles, illness are all the result of the inner evil power of sin. And we have all sinned and fallen short of God's glory...no human is any better than another in that regard.

159

Does God Care What Happens To Me?   *Chapter Nine*

Sin separates us from God. He will not fellowship with sin or sinners. God does not fellowship with any form of rebellion against Himself. This separation is referred to in the Bible as "spiritual death".

It's a difficult thing for human beings to comprehend… that God has turned His back against the plight and anguish of a sinner…even though God still loves the sinner. But this is our situation. We are alone, without any Godly support, while we continue to rebel against the authority and love of our Creator.

And this separation from God will last for eternity. God will not allow sin or sinners to be part of His eternal Kingdom. You and I have rebelled against our Creator, to commit sin, and we are doomed to be eternally separated from Him. This is precisely what God's authoritative word (the Bible) teaches us.

Is there an answer to this tragic situation of mankind? Fortunately … yes! The answer is … remove sin from the earth and all our problems immediately disappear. Life is actually that basic and simple. Our only hope individually, nationally and internationally is that we be delivered from the power of sin that dominates every human life…but how?

Nothing in our human capacity can resolve the problem of sin. Science, education, politics, social and economic status …nor our mental and physical health professions…can remove the sin within each one of us. Even "religion" is incompetent to resolve the problem of the sinner.

160

Does God Care What Happens To Me?   *Chapter Nine*

But the Bible has the answer, as it reveals another role that God has assumed for Himself in behalf of our human family. It is the role of "Savior" whereby we may be delivered (saved) from sin's power.

"Salvation comes from God. He gives joy to all his people."   Psalm 3:8

"For God so loved the world, that he gave his only begotten Son, that whosoever believeth in him should not perish, but have everlasting life. For God sent not his Son into the world to condemn the world; but that the world through him might be saved. He that believeth on Him is not condemned: but he that believeth not is condemned already, because he hath not believed in the name of the only begotten Son of God. And this is the condemnation, that light is come into the world, and men loved darkness rather than light, because their deeds were evil. For every one that doeth evil hateth the light, neither cometh to the light, lest his deeds should be reproved.. But he that doeth truth cometh to the light, that his deeds may be made manifest, that they are wrought in God."   John 3:3-21

"If we confess our sins, he is faithful and just to forgive us our sins, and to cleanse us from all unrighteousness."

1 John 1:9

161

CONCLUSION

The Bible reveals a God of love who desires to have an intimate relationship with His creation. The first two human beings, Adam and Eve, were placed on an earth where everything was good and perfect. No evil existed...only a perfect union between God and His creation. The earth was a literal paradise. Adam and Eve were "eternal" beings who would live forever in the fellowship and presence of God. The relationship between God and His human creation was perfect.

Then tragedy struck and the results continue to this day. A tempter came to Adam and Eve with a message that they also could be gods...that they did not need God...that God was only trying to rule and dictate over them. They listened to the tempter, to rebel against God...and the rest is history.

Adam and Eve had become sinners...rebellious and disobedient to their Creator. The results were staggering. They were expelled from God's presence and fellowship. The world no longer would be the paradise that God had designed for them.

Their offspring would inherit their rebellious nature; to follow in their sinful footsteps...and mankind was reduced to being a mere mortal who would experience physical death.

Man and woman desired to exist without the Creator, so God stepped aside to let them try. Our human failures and calamities have proven how terrible the choice has been.

Does God Care What Happens To Me?   *Chapter Nine*

But the good news is ...God is real and God is love. God is interested in your life and mine. God knows everything we face in this life. Sometimes we must suffer pain because of life's evils...but we do not suffer alone.

Our Heavenly Father is a close companion who will never allow anything to overtake us...no matter how severe the trouble may be. We are more than conquerors through Him who loves us.

Where else in this life is there a greater hope or more certain assurance than God? He is available to all those who seek Him...and the best is yet to come. We are promised a life in Heaven where evil will never again intrude.

Paul said it well when he offered this insight... "If in this world only, we have hope, we are of all men most miserable."

But then again he said... " I know in whom I have believed and am persuaded that He (God) is able to keep that which have committed unto Him against that day."

Does God involve Himself in the affairs of a single human being? You better believe it! I speak for millions of people when I say...God has never failed me as I place my complete trust in His goodness and mercy.

Everywhere we look, reality just keeps getting better and better.

What You Can Expect From God   *Chapter Ten*

Ready For Some More
Really Great News...?

Hi, it's me again...Ken Howard...the guy who wrote the stuff you've been reading in this little book. I hope you have found me to be upfront and honest with you so far...that I've been trying to pass along some useful information that can help make a positive difference in your life.

As we close this discussion I would like to reveal some personal things about myself to let you know that real humans do experience some miraculous things in their lives that can be credited only to God's kind intervention.

People ask me in counseling sessions and seminars, "Do you really believe in the Bible and do you believe that God is interested enough to become involved in my life?" They were actually asking ..."Do you have any experience to back up your beliefs?" Head knowledge alone doesn't get the job done!

To answer those who may have similar questions I submit the following personal experiences that happened just as they are recorded here. As I share these experiences you should know that I am suspicious of personal reports of "miracles" and "visions"....just as I am sure you are. But I cannot shy away from that which I personally know to be absolutely true.

164

What You Can Expect From God   **Chapter Ten**

Do true miracles happen and does God really get involved with the ordinary events of our life? You be the judge from what you are about to read.

The following true experiences are shared as my effort to set on record the evidence that God does intervene in behalf of our human family...and that even in these difficult times in which we live there is Divine help and hope for every situation.

I share these experiences with the hope that they will be an encouragement for you. No one is more special to God than you are...and every need of your life is as much a concern to God as are the needs of every other human being. God is capable, willing and available to help in your most difficult of circumstance. There is no problem without an answer and there is no situation without hope. I know from experience.

My problem is in deciding what experiences to include in this short writing, for I have many events to share. God's interventions throughout my adult life can only be described as remarkable, to say the least...beyond human understanding. I still stand in awe as I bring each one to memory.

I do not regard myself to be distinctly deserving of God's attention beyond others of my human family...for it is my belief that every human being is loved of God and that His resources are available to everyone. The few experiences that I share are not the result of anything I have done to earn them, but rather the results of God's merciful grace in behalf of my need.

165

What You Can Expect From God   *Chapter Ten*

I've selected four miracles to share from the long list of miracles that have occurred to me personally. But first, let me define a miracle from God as I understand it to be and how it is used in this writing.

A MIRACLE OF GOD DEFINED

A miracle of God is something that happens without any human intervention...a "special visitation" of God beyond the normal and natural processes of nature, science or human expertise. A miracle is something that God performs in an individual's life that cannot be explained any other way.

A "miracle of God" should be distinguished from other "miracles", in that a special visitation from God takes place in behalf of human need.

Each event you are about to read involved a special visitation from God without any human involvement to supply a special need in my life.

WHERE I'M COMING FROM

Simply stated, I am a human being like other human beings...a person who God loves and who God desires to help. I have a normal family life, I've seen both the good and the bad times and I make mistakes. I have an extensive college education and a professional background. I regard myself to be well educated, stable and clear thinking.

What You Can Expect From God   Chapter Ten

I am identified professionally to be an all disciplines certified researcher, a human behavioral scientist, a private counseling Psychologist, a marriage and family counselor, a corporate employee referral counselor, a law enforcement stress management advisor, a theologian, a student of history, a college professor, a seminar speaker, a husband of one wife, a father of three daughters (all grown)...and I own my own home and cut my own grass.

I also do woodworking as a hobby...and I've been known to take the controls of an airplane, to do a few stalls and spins every now and then. Whew...maybe I should think about retiring (at least from grass cutting)!

I've never been a "religious" person in the context of being a devotee or supporter of any specific religion or denominational group of human origin...including the "religion of Christianity". I've not seen the need in my life to become a member of organized religion.

In other words, I am not a "Protestant" or "Catholic"... nor do I endorse any ancient or eastern religions that are popular with New Age ideologies. I am, however, a believer and follower of Jesus Christ and His teachings.

My faith and allegiance to Christ have been determined by the irrefutable scientific and historical evidence that proves Jesus is indeed the true Messiah from God...as well as by the numerous miracles I have received through Him.

167

What You Can Expect From God   *Chapter Ten*

I am an average person who has experienced some extraordinary and miraculous events in my life, as I learned to open myself up to the fellowship of God. The events you are about to read are true. I begin with the most powerful of all miracles…a complete change of character that occurred in an instant moment of time.

THE MIRACLE OF A NEW LIFE WITH GOD

I married right out of high school and started college and a family at the same time. My first college major was business. I landed an office job with a major paper manufacturer where I was trained and primed for executive responsibilities. I was in the right place at the right time. One of the company's top executives took me under his wing and I was in a position of unlimited advancement even at a very young age. My responsibilities and paycheck continued to grow. Life was good. We bought our first home, enjoyed the niceties and became involved in community projects. I became a pilot and was considering the purchase of a private airplane. I loved to fly.

I was young, proud and healthy. I had been active in sports throughout my life and continued to play in basketball and baseball leagues. I needed nothing. I was in total control. Things could not have been better. It was then that my life was turned upside down, never again to be the same.

What You Can Expect From God   *Chapter Ten*

One evening while sitting at home I picked up a Bible that someone had given us and opened it to page one. That simple event started a chain of events that led to the most profound experience I have ever had.

I had never bothered to read the Bible before, so I figured it would be something different to glance through. I attribute my curiosity to the faithfulness of my mother who had seen to it that I attended church and Sunday school as a child.

As I began reading at the beginning it didn't take me long to get to "Cain's wife". Where in the world did Cain get His wife? If Adam and Eve were the only two people on earth and they had only two sons, Cain and Abel, then where did Cain's wife come from? Was she an alien from another planet...or is the Bible accurate? This really confused me.

Days went by and I couldn't get the idea of Cain's wife off my mind. My curiosity was highly exaggerated, something out of character for me. I consulted an expert...my grandmother. This was a mistake (actually a blessing) for this was another link that changed my life forever.

I had known for years that my grandmother possessed a special gift of faith and that she was well educated on the Bible. The lady simply knew how to pray to get her prayers answered.

My phone call triggered my grandmother's brain that I was showing an interest in "spiritual" matters. No I wasn't! I just wanted to know where Cain's wife came from.

169

What You Can Expect From God   **Chapter Ten**

My life was in good shape and I was very busy. God wasn't important to me. I was getting along just fine without God, so I thought. Maybe I had a few faults but I wasn't as bad as some people I knew. I worked hard, supported my family, did my community stuff...yet there was this occasional twinge of guilt that something was missing.

But, all I wanted was to know "where Cain's wife come from?" yet this dear grandmother decided to pray for my spiritual needs...the result being that my life went into total chaos. Life had been good until then but that was to quickly change. All of the sudden, for the first time in my life, I began to feel guilty and fearful of an approaching punishment. I felt dirty, ugly and sinful. The guilt and fear were so intense that I could not sleep or perform my duties.

I began to experience chest pains and shortness of breath. My whole thought was consumed with dying and going to hell. I did not want to die and be eternally punished. I couldn't go to sleep at night for fear I would die. I couldn't function during the day for fear I would die. Flying was no longer a joy for me but I was still required to travel in my work. The fear of death and hell were so great that I was literally drenched in sweat from takeoff to landing. On one occasion I canceled a flight from New York that would have taken me home in a few hours, opting instead to travel all night by train ...because trains don't fall out of the sky to kill people.

170

What You Can Expect From God   *Chapter Ten*

I knew I was having a heart attack...that some terrible disease had invaded my body...that I was going to suddenly die. I consulted with a physician for a complete physical exam. It proved how healthy I was, yet the physician recognized my mental condition to prescribe medication. He assumed it to be job or family related stress. I dared not tell him of my desperate fear of death and hell for fear he would think I was a religious basket case.

I became dissatisfied with life, with my job and with my family. Nothing pleased me anymore. Life was lousy. I decided to quit my job to the dismay of my employer. They couldn't imagine a young man giving up the promising career that was inevitable for me. I was being primed for top executive position. My future was assured...but I was still going to die and go to hell. I quit my job, took another, and quit that job also in less than a month. I didn't realize while all this was going on that it was God dealing with me...that He was being merciful to me.

It was at this point in my life that the most profound miracle I have ever experienced took place. It began when my red Ford took on a mind of its own one June Friday morning.

I was driving to a business appointment with that on my mind. Suddenly my red Ford stopped. I found myself sitting in the middle of an empty church parking lot. What happened? I did not drive my car into the parking lot. I did not want to park here. I wanted to go to a business meeting.

171

What You Can Expect From God　　　　　　　　*Chapter Ten*

I said to myself, "Ken, you are out of your mind. What in the world are you doing? Get this thing started and get to your meeting." That's when a voice spoke to me..."Get out of the car and go into the church". Remarkably I obeyed and went to the door...but it was locked. I walked all around the church and every door was locked. No one was there that early on a Friday morning. Thinking how ridiculous this was I walked back to the car, but the voice again spoke..."Return to the church and I will open the door for you." I did so and was shocked when the locked door flew open of its own accord.

I walked in and found myself in the rear of the sanctuary of a large church, looking toward the front at the pulpit and altars. This was the first time I had been inside a church in years. The church was empty except for two ministers who were standing at the altar...waiting for me. One of the ministers, who knew my parents and family, looked up as I entered. He recognized me. As I walked toward him I was rehearsing in my mind what I would say as to the reason I was there in church on a Friday morning. As he reached out to shake my hand I broke down and began to weep. I found myself crying out, "Pastor, I need to be saved."...Whatever that meant I did not then know.

With that, he and the other minister and myself knelt down at an altar of prayer where I began to pray that God would be merciful to forgive my sins. I needed no pastoral counseling. I was not looking to join a church or religion. All I wanted was

172

What You Can Expect From God   **Chapter Ten**

to be free from the burden of guilt and fear that was haunting me day and night. I wanted my life to be better than what it was.

It was then that the most profound miracle I have ever experienced took place. As I prayed, God entered into my life... but how do you explain an experience like that with words?

In just a few moments of time my life was totally changed. My whole character and outlook were instantly converted to see life as God sees it...even though I knew very little about spiritual things. The guilt and fear that I had been carrying around for years immediately vanished. They were replaced with a peace and joy that I had never before experienced and which remains to this day. I felt totally clean and pure for the first time in my life.

The heavy burden that had been my constant companion had been lifted. Life was not only good again...it was great. I had come into the presence of God. I had experienced His love and forgiveness...and His cleansing. I knew that there was no longer anything between my Creator and me, and that I had been accepted into His Kingdom. My entire sinful past had been miraculously forgiven and erased from God's memory.

I later came to realize that what I had experienced on that Friday morning in June was a spiritual surgery performed by God known as being "born again". Sin had miraculously been cut away and had been replaced with the righteousness of God.

173

What You Can Expect From God   Chapter Ten

I had been released from the evil power that had control of my life and which had caused me to deny and reject God. I no longer felt guilty or dirty or fearful. I felt clean and loved and accepted.

In an instant of time I had become a child of God and was now part of His family, never again to be alone or without hope. I walked out of the church that day a new man. Everything appeared brighter...life, the trees, the flowers... everything.

The first hard evidence that something miraculous had happened was my shirt pocket. That's where a packet of cigarettes always lived. I dropped the pack in the first trash bin I came to and then another miracle happened. Although I had tried unsuccessfully on several occasions to quit my two-pack-a-day habit...from that moment to this I never again had a desire or craving for another cigarette...not even a passing thought. And the same was true with alcohol, which was becoming more than just social drinking on business trips.

But there was much more than that to come. My entire attitude and outlook about life had miraculously changed. The God I had shunned while I pursued my life was now my entire focus. I wanted to become acquainted with Him and to experience His presence. The truths within the Bible began to open up to me as I devoured the reading of it. I was no longer afraid or confused about life and death. The warmth and embrace of God were now my constant companions.

What You Can Expect From God   *Chapter Ten*

The miracle of my spiritual "rebirth" was far greater and more effective than what any personal resolution could have achieved. It was an instantaneous experience that completely removed all the things that were wrong, to replace them with all the things that were right.

The results are history. That miracle happened 35 years ago to become the beginning of the rest of my life. The joy and peace remain to this day as I continue to enjoy God's continuing presence...where His love and assurance to me, that all is well, is the foundation of my life.

The miracle of that day was the result of a simple, yet sincere prayer. I had reached a point in my life of realizing that my sins were my whole problem, and that my only hope was to seek forgiveness and deliverance from them. God saw my sincerity and heard my prayer. He did the rest...to perform a spiritual miracle that "religion" is incapable of doing.

I soon came to realize that the reason my prayer was heard and my sins forgiven had nothing to do with my ability to change... or that I had any influence with God. I had no ability to change my life nor did I have any influence with God.

I was like every other human being who has ever lived. I had sinned and failed in the eyes of God, and my sins had separated me from Him. I had nothing to offer or to bargain with. I was a sinner whose sins must be punished. But the good news is...no human being, needs to fear the punishment for sin.

175

What You Can Expect From God   *Chapter Ten*

Our punishment was taken by another person, who sacrificed Himself so that our sins could be forgiven...if that is what we desire. God's son, Jesus the Christ, died as a sacrifice for our sins...so that our prayers for forgiveness can be heard and our relationship with God restored.

My prayer was heard, my sins forgiven and my life totally changed because of Jesus, who now lives at the right hand of God as our intercessor...our Messiah. God listens and answers our prayers, not for anything we have done, but only because of what Jesus Christ has done for us. Jesus said it this way, "I am the way, the truth and the life...no man comes to the Father but by me."

What I have just told you is true. I'm not the only person whose life has been miraculously changed by the kind and merciful intervention of our Creator. Millions of other people can share a similar story that transformed their life in a miraculous way.

A SPECIAL VISITATION AND MIRACLE
OF PHYSICAL HEALING

I must confess that I am very skeptical of modern-day "faith healers" who preach a wealth and health gospel. But I am not skeptical of God's ability or desire to heal His people...for I have so been healed on several occasions. Many other people

176

What You Can Expect From God   **Chapter Ten**

have also testified to similar healings where God intervened without the help of medicine or physicians. One of the more serious situations and blessing was the miraculous healing of terminal cancer...yet the healing was only a small part of the real blessing of that experience.

The doctors and laboratory tests had diagnosed me with a terminal cancer of the most serious kind. There was, and still is, no known cure for this specific type of cancer. The only possible hope was surgery to remove the disease, although once it had invaded the blood stream there was no hope even with surgery. We had no other option, surgery was hastily scheduled.

My hospital room was semi-private with an elderly dying man in the other bed. My family and friends had left for the night and the nursing staff had completed my pre-op for next day surgery. Only a small table light had been left on and the door to our room was closed so that I might get some rest from the hallway noise.

I was alone. For the first time since the cancer diagnosis I was alone with my thoughts of what I was dealing with. I began to pray, but my prayer was not for mercy or healing. Although I don't recall the precise wording, I prayed something like this... "Lord, for the first time in my life I face the reality of possible death as the result of this disease. If that be your will, so be it. I am grateful for the life you have given me and whether I live of die, I shall serve you."

What You Can Expect From God   *Chapter Ten*

Then the miracle happened just as I now describe it. Suddenly the door to my room opened. It was a heavy door with a self-closing hinge that kept it shut unless propped open. As I lay there watching I realized that no one had opened it, but that the door had opened of its own accord.

Then God walked in. God was not in human form nor did I see a physical image, but God's presence was so powerful that I followed Him step-by-step as He walked from the door to the side of my bed.

It is impossible to describe with mere words the presence that had entered my room. I looked up into the presence of God standing by my bed and I felt His arms encircle me. I felt safe and secure, and at total peace.

Although there was no physical form to see, I knew that I was in the presence of God. I saw Him and heard Him speak with my "spiritual eyes and ears". I was not hallucinating or dreaming. I had not been given any drugs or relaxation pills nor was I hooked up to any equipment or IV's. It was just God and me.

I felt His embrace just as a father would embrace a child who needs assurance and comfort. Then I heard Him speak.

God's voice was not audible yet very clear and decisive. I have heard that same voice numerous times throughout my adult life. It is a voice unmistakable, yet indescribable. The words spoken to me were to this effect...

What You Can Expect From God   *Chapter Ten*

"I have removed the disease that has invaded your body. You are totally healed. You will not die in surgery tomorrow or any other time from this disease." Then He was gone.

Had God told me to get dressed and leave, that there was no longer the need for surgery, I would have done so…for I knew at that moment I was totally healed. But for whatever reason I do not know…I was still to undergo surgery.

Maybe the surgery was for the benefit of the doctors and my family, who were not privileged to this private visitation from God, to confirm my healing for them.

The surgery went as planned. The lab results told the whole story… "Ken, we have some great news. Not only is there no evidence of the cancer spreading, but the previously infected parts are clean as well."

Simply stated, the scars of more than one hundred stitches in my body need not be here. The surgery accomplished nothing other than as evidence that the great Surgeon had already operated the night before.

That experience left me with a wonderful memory of God's love and mercy that I know He extends to all His children. The great blessing for me was not the healing of a terminal cancer, but rather that God would honor me with His presence and personal visit.

There is no greater blessing than to experience a fellowship with God.

What You Can Expect From God **Chapter Ten**

I've enjoyed other physical healings from the Lord over the years, as has my wife and our children...and every experience reminds us of our Heavenly Father's love and mercy. We also have been privileged to participate in and witness miraculous physical healing of other people, which cannot be explained in mere human understanding.

BUT, APPARENTLY, GOD IS INTERESTED
IN OTHER THINGS BEYOND SAVING SOULS
AND HEALING BODIES

Boy, I sure hope this next story doesn't come across as some fanatic with a yarn to spin. It's about the miraculous healing of an old Rambler transmission. Even my own mother didn't want me to tell this story in such a classy book as this...although she knows it really happened just as I'm about to tell you.

For those of you too young to remember...a Rambler was a car...and even way back in 1964 they made cars with automatic transmissions. When I finally bought the old used Rambler years later, that transmission had been shifted a whole, whole bunch of times.

I've learned over the years that God is interested in every area of our life, both minor and major, to help in situations where things appear to be impossible. The healing of a

What You Can Expect From God   *Chapter Ten*

transmission at a time when my family really needed God's help was one of those occasions. That may sound exaggerated or fanatical, but read on, for this miracle of God happened just as I describe it.

It happened while I was in college with only one car for school and work. My family was very young then...a wife, three daughters (one in diapers). We had all sacrificed for me to continue my education, which we felt the Lord wanted me to pursue. I was working on the freight docks at night to pay our living and school expenses. We always had enough to pay the rent and buy groceries but nothing was left to sock back for "emergencies". Those were left to prayer.

One emergency was the old 1964 Rambler. It had an automatic transmission that did what it was supposed to. When you pointed the gearshift to the "D", it drove forward...and when you pointed it to the "R", it reversed. Life was good. Then the unspeakable happened. One day as I hopped in the old Rambler to go to work, I put it in "R" to get out of the driveway...but it didn't "R". So I put it in "D"...but it wouldn't "D" either. The old faithful Rambler just sat there and purred. I assumed it had to be something with the transmission since kicking the tires didn't get it moving. I was right.

Some friends helped me tow it to the transmission expert. He checked it out and gave me the bad news. The transmission was totally shot...no other option but to buy a new

181

What You Can Expect From God   **Chapter Ten**

one. I asked the urgent question, "How much?" The news wasn't good there either. A new transmission back then went for the gargantuan price of $180 bucks.

"180 dollars? ", I yelled! "I'm in college, I got a family...I don't have 180 cents, let on a 180 dollars." But my appeal didn't draw any sympathy. "No skin off my back", said the expert, "If you want it fixed, it's $180". So I did the honorable thing, I towed the sick old Rambler back home and kicked the tires again, this time in disgust.

I announced the bad news to my wife who was knee deep in sweat from folding diapers in the hot, non air-conditioned, roach infested mansion we were renting. Our three little girls weren't smiling either. So I tried to get the Rambler running again. No success. It wouldn't "D" or "R". It was dead in the water. We were shipwrecked. No sail, no rudder, no movement, no nothing.

That's when the wife suggested, "If God can heal souls and God can heal bodies, don't you imagine that He could heal a Rambler transmission?" Hmmmm....you don't suppose.....?

That's when one big guy, a cute wife, and three little girls were seen laying their hands on the hood of a 1964 Rambler, with heads bowed as our family agreed in prayer.... "God, please heal our transmission. Amen". Then the miracle happened...God showed up.

182

What You Can Expect From God   **Chapter Ten**

Back in the Rambler I crawled, put the key in the ignition and started the engine. Then I put the lever in "D". The Rambler lunged forward like it was supposed to do! I put the lever in "R". The Rambler went backward like it was supposed to do! Our Rambler was healed! Once again God had come to the aide of His children. The girls all felt that we should take a test drive and recommended the grueling trip all the way to the ice cream shop. And since we were there they felt it in our best interest to have an ice cream...just to calm the trauma we had been through. Best money I ever spent.

The Rambler lasted all the time we remained in school and even after we returned home to Ohio where we later traded it in for another used car. It wouldn't surprise me if that old Rambler passed us up one day heading somewhere north on I-75, still with the same transmission.

And then there's the time God miraculously healed an old Ford way out west on highway I-70, that time on the electrical system that had us totally shipwrecked, sitting on the side of an interstate without any help. But that's another story for another time.

These were not the only times that God came to our family's rescue in a miraculous way. The list of God's interventions in seeing to our physical and financial needs is a long one that spans throughout our life. We've moved around the country, lived in almost every conceivable situation,

What You Can Expect From God   **Chapter Ten**

experienced both the good and the tough times…yet our needs were always supplied. We've witnessed God's miracles with all kinds of financial need, yet financial and physical help are not the only things that God has provided for us. He also has delivered us from imminent danger on various occasions, one of which I include in this writing.

GOD'S MIRACULOUS DELIVERANCE
FROM A REBEL GANG

During the time when I was in college in Houston, Texas there were certain sections of the downtown area where you did not want to find yourself late at night, especially alone. But there I was, alone in a deserted, dark alleyway, separated from my friends in the late, late hours of the night…or wee, wee hours of the morning (whichever).

It isn't important what we were doing there at that time of night or how I became separated from my friends, other than to say that we weren't there for any illegal or immoral reasons.

Suddenly a gang of men surrounded me. Each had a knife in one hand and a bottle of liquor in the other. The look on their faces told my fate even before they began to speak. I had never before, or since then, seen such hatred in human eyes. I was a dead man. I would not leave that alleyway alive.

184

What You Can Expect From God   *Chapter Ten*

One of the men stood nose to nose with me, reeking of sweat and alcohol...and hate. I actually smelled his animosity and loathing toward me although I had never before met the man. His eyes glared into mine as he challenged me with a simple invitation ..."Talk to me, man". I heard the snickers and laughter from the others as they anticipated what they were about to do.

I began to talk. To this day I have no idea what I said or how long I spoke, but amazingly I had no fear. As I began to speak an awesome miracle took place. The presence of God came down like an invisible protective shield all around me.

God's presence was so evident that the expression on the men's faces began to change. They began to mellow and slump like little kittens. Their eyes no longer glared with defiance and hatred, but were now filled with tears as they began to cry. They backed away a few steps to give me room to speak. Their knives and liquor had dropped to the ground. Their jaws had sagged, their mouths wide open in total amazement.

Something miraculous was happening beyond human capacity or understanding. The love of God was being poured into their hearts from heaven itself. It was probably the first time any of them had ever been exposed to God's presence where perfect love is manifested. In just a few moments of time God changed those violent men from potential murderers to passive

185

What You Can Expect From God   *Chapter Ten*

spectators of His presence. Rather than putting a knife into my flesh they each put their hands out to shake mine.

Their last words to me were something to the effect that "they had never before witnessed anything like what had just happened ...that I had something they didn't and that they would be giving serious thought to what they heard and witnessed that night." With that they left. I got a hunch I'll see a couple of those guys in heaven some day.

The love of God was so powerful in that Houston alleyway that it caused the most defiant agents of hate to surrender to it. I witnessed how hardened, militant men must succumb to the love of God and how that God protects His children even in the most perilous of circumstance. Yes, I know that the disciples of Christ, including the apostle Paul, all gave their lives for their testimony. There have been many throughout history who were tortured and persecuted for their faith...but there have also been great times of deliverance as in that Houston alleyway...for whatever reason God so willed.

I was delivered from certain death because God once again visited with me. He wasn't quite done with my life yet.

There have been other experiences of God's protective grace that delivered me from danger and death...each of which serves as a certain reminder to me that the promise of God stands true... "I will never leave or forsake you, but will go with you to the ends of the earth".

What You Can Expect From God   **Chapter Ten**

I can't imagine going through life without Him. Our family is deeply grateful for the visits of God and for His many interventions in our behalf for healing, for protection, for provision and for deliverance. Yet none compares with the profound miracle that happened to me around 10:00 a.m. on a Friday morning in June, 1965. At that moment I experienced a spiritual miracle that removed the fear and guilt of my sinful past to replace them with a pure peace and joy that remains to this day. In an instant moment of time I became a child of God that started a life-long relationship with a loving Heavenly Father that continues to this day.

At this writing I continue to enjoy the benefits of life and health ...and to experience God's visits and assurance. God meets every need of His children. We can verify with certainty that God is not slack concerning His promises. He will do what He has promised.

Many years ago my wife and I took for ourselves His promise to "Seek first the Kingdom of God and His righteousness and all your needs will be supplied." (Mat 6:33) We did our part and God has certainly done His.

There are numerous other experiences that I would very much like to share with you someday, possibly at another writing or in person. I have learned from my own experiences and the experiences of others, that in matters of financial need, physical need, emotional need, spiritual need and any other

What You Can Expect From God   **Chapter Ten**

need…God is loving and merciful to supply our need beyond what we can ever imagine.

But beyond the many miracles that God is capable and willing to perform in our behalf, the greatest blessing in life is to experience His love and presence. Nothing compares with the privilege of having a personal and intimate relationship with our Creator. Knowing that miracles do happen…that's encouraging. Knowing that miracles can happen for you…that's hope. But knowing the "Miracle Maker"…that's what life is all about.

These personal experiences happened just as I described them. I've learned in my years of fellowship with God that everything in the Bible is true and accurate and that all His promises of an abundant and happy life here on earth are real…even when life's situations are sometimes painful and threatening and challenging.

Life has been very good for me…because of God. I am deeply and humbly grateful for all that the Lord has done in my behalf and in behalf of my family. And the best is yet to come…God has promised that His followers shall someday leave the pain and suffering of this world to live eternally with Him.

Because Jesus lives forever…we shall also live forever in the full and joyous presence of God…where sin, sorrow and pain do not exist. I'm not sure what heaven will be like…but where God is, there shall be peace, righteousness and eternal

What You Can Expect From God   *Chapter Ten*

joy. Heaven is all that this world cannot be. The benefits are worth the trip. I don't want to miss it.

I thank you for taking the time to read this simple account of my experiences with God. It is my prayer that you will receive some hope and strength from something that has been shared. You are an important person to God. He is interested in your life and the things that are happening with you.

Whatever your past has been...it is not as important to God as what your future can be. God is no "respecter of persons"... What He has done for me and for millions of others...He will do for you. My prayers are with you.

Your friend who loves you,

Ken Howard

**The Author And His Colleagues**

Dr. Kenneth W. Howard

SO, WHO AM I ...

...that I would assume to have some information that could be beneficial to you?

Before we talk about me, let's look at some of my friends who contributed to these studies. When it comes to the topic of "life", there is no one person with all the answers.

I am very fortunate to have access to some of the most brilliant minds and researchers on the planet. Somewhere in these studies I've had to call upon the wisdom of physical scientists, astronomers, biologists, chemists, historians, medical researchers, theologians, mathematicians, behavioral experts... and a lot of common sense.

As for me, I have been a student, counselor and teacher on the topic of life for more years than I wish to admit. The previous chapter identifies my true credentials for this writing, but just in case you need some scholarly and professional certification, here's where I'm coming from.

I attended seven universities, majoring in three disciplines...Business, Theology and Psychology. I am licensed in all 50 states as a "healing professional". I have a private

The Author And His Colleagues

counseling practice where I counsel people (by referral) who have really bad problems. I deal with Corporations in their EAP programs; Police Agencies with stress management; Ministers and Churches with marriage, family and spiritual issues; Social Service groups with psychological and social traumas; etc., etc.

I am expected to identify the problem, sort out all the confusion, suggest a realistic remedy, and encourage those who have been beat down with life. It's a great job!

Then there's this research stuff I have to do. I'm supposed to know a little about everything (so they say). My research background spans physical science, ancient and modern history, sociology, Bible and theology, humanities, physics, biology, chemistry, astrophysics, astronomy, world religions, mental health, philosophy...and elephant jokes.

Of all the research I've done over many years, there is no greater wisdom that has come to my attention than that which is recorded in the book we call the Bible. And I say that as a person who is not a member of any organized religious group.

I lecture and teach to special interest groups around the country. I've taught college classes and have been asked to do a weekly national television broadcast, but I declined.

Then, there's this woman I met in high school and married many years ago. She also helps to keep me straight (since she always gets in the last word)...naturally! And she has the greatest kids and grandkids you would ever want to meet.

The Author And His Colleagues

Finally, I pray a lot. I've learned that knowledge can be gained through study and experience...but wisdom in how to use that knowledge comes only from our omniscient Creator.

So, what do I do for fun? I got a little woodshop at my house where I make stuff. I'd pilot airplanes more often if the little lady (mentioned above) didn't expect me to keep both feet on the ground. And, yep, I enjoy all the college and professional sports (what guy with hair on his chest doesn't).

But the family always comes first...there's no hobby more important than people...at least for me. That's who I am.

ENDORSEMENTS and ACCOLADES

So far, every member of my family and all our friends who have read the book totally endorse it and give it their thumbs up. Of course, you knew they would, didn't you?

I have not approached my professional colleagues and some high-profile people I know to endorse this book. In all honesty, I don't think endorsements have any value. I've never seen an endorsement in a book that doesn't say something nice ...so what's the point? Must be my southern heritage!

FINALLY, I AM A VERY HONEST PERSON
WHO WILL ALWAYS TELL YOU THE TRUTH
AS BEST AS I UNDERSTAND IT

Other Books In This Series

Answers And More

The Book Series

Courtesy Of

Dr. Kenneth W. Howard and Colleagues

We are deeply concerned at the great amount of spiritual and social ignorance in this day of imaginary "intellectual enlightenment". A lack of exposure to scientific, historical and Biblical truth in the developmental childhood years, while being taught false science and moral confusion in the educational system, has distorted the reality of human purpose and value.

Further, the distorted messages of secularist life styles, religious confusion and New Age philosophies have created uncertainty and skepticism toward any religious principles.

As a consequence, the current "enlightened" generation is totally ignorant and unprepared to deal with life in a realistic way. They see human life as a non-value, to develop disrespect for their Creator, for themselves, for other human beings, and for the physical environment in which we are dependent for survival. The results are apparent in every shocking newscast.

For many, hope is lost, while depression and frustration take control. We want to help by sharing some positive reality.

Other Books In This Series

FIRST TITLES IN THIS SERIES

Book One

Your Life And Beyond

Who am I? Where did I come from?

Why am I here? Where am I headed?

Book Two

The God Of Creation

Can God be trusted? Does God care what happens to me?

What proof is there that God exists? Who is the real God?

Book Three

True Meaningful Religion

What is religion and being religious? What is spirituality?

Why are there so many different religions? Who is right?

How can I find truth for myself?

How can any religion be trusted after all the evils they've done?

Does a person have to belong to a religion to find God?

Other Books In This Series

Book Four
The Final Days Of Mankind

Is the world really coming to an end?

Haven't prophets predicted the world's end for centuries?

Is the Bible really 100% accurate in prophesying future events?

Has the final pre-sign date now occurred?

What signs are we to look for to the world's end?

Book Five
The Problem Of God And Evil

Who is at fault for all the human suffering?

Where did evil come from?

Why do the good and innocent people suffer?

Why doesn't God do something to help us?

**More titles are also coming soon to your bookstores and
retail outlets. For more information on how to order any of
these titles by mail, write to....**

Direction, Inc.

P.O. Box 213

Middletown, Ohio 45042

E-Mail: direct@siscom.net

website: http://www.answersandmore.com

Bibliography

The references for this study are so extensive that a listing of all of them would be impractical and would require this book to be twice the size that it is.

You may obtain a complete list of references by written request to:

Kenneth W. Howard, PhD

Direction, Inc.

PO Box 213

Middletown, Ohio   45042

For a partial list, you may visit our website at:

http://www.answersandmore.com